The New Work of Our Hands

The New

Mae Rockland Tupa

Work of Our Hands

Contemporary Jewish Needlework and Quilts

CHILTON BOOK COMPANY   Radnor, Pennsylvania

Designed by Tracy Baldwin

All photographs by Susan E. Byrne, except where otherwise credited

All illustrations, textile projects and designs by Mae Rockland Tupa
unless otherwise credited

Manufactured in the United States of America

Library of Congress Cataloging in Publication Data

Tupa, Mae Rockland.
    The new work of our hands: contemporary Jewish needlework and
quilts / Mae Rockland Tupa. — 2nd ed.
        p.   cm.
    Rev. ed. of: The work of our hands. 1973.
    Includes bibliographical references and index.
    ISBN 0-8019-8362-2
    1. Needlework, Jewish. 2. Patchwork. I. Tupa, Mae Rockland.
Work of our hands. II. Title.
TT750.T86   1994
764.44′089′924—dc20   93-33135
                                                                CIP

1 2 3 4 5 6 7 8 9 0   2 1 0 9 8 7 6 5 4

For Keren Chaya:

To be a child is to know the excitement of life

To have a daughter is to know the meaning of life

CONTENTS

PREFACE

Twenty years ago when I began writing my first book, *The Work of Our Hands: Jewish Needlecraft for Today*, I said, "What is currently available in crafts for Jewish-Americans, either to buy or to make, is paltry indeed. If we go looking for a *matzoh* or *hallah* cover to buy, we find that the only objects available are far below even Green Stamp standards. . . . If we are truly interested in enriching our aesthetic and religious lives simultaneously, we shall have to make the things ourselves."

It certainly seems as though many people felt as frustrated with the paucity of fine and fun Judaica as I did, because over the last two decades, even as we have been struggling with the ambivalences of assimilation that plague a free society, we have been producing splendid Judaica artifacts in all media. This is as true of textiles as of clay, wood, metal, stone, paint, and canvas.

When I sent out a letter asking craftspeople to tell me what they have been doing and to send pictures, I was fairly inundated with wonderful and exciting work. Unfortunately, I can only show here a small percentage of this bounty. I've included as much as there was room for, bringing you a variety of objects and motifs in different styles and techniques. Because the emphasis of this book is on needlework and quilts I have left out some marvelous examples of woven and painted textiles. More often then not they were the work of professional artists, using techniques and equipment that are not easily available to the amateur needle maven for whom this book is written. Because there are many books available with technical how-to information, I've chosen to devote these pages to presenting as much inspirational material as possible, as well as line patterns for symbols and alef-bets. How you use them is up to you. I would, in fact, love to see your renditions of the designs shown here.

My letter also raised various questions of political correctness. Is needlework "craft" or "art?" Because mainly women are involved with it, and women have had such a raw deal, we'd better call it "art." But I have a problem with this tendency to generalize. There are wonderful things being made. There are awful things being made. "Art" is not automatically better than "craft." This book will ignore that particular issue. Is ritual art "folk art" or art-art? How can Jews have "folk" art when we are primarily an urban people and don't have cows and chickens handy, except in the supermarket? Well, we are the only folks we have, and when ordinary people use the materials that are available to them and the very best of their skills to make objects or images for their own use and enjoyment, *that* is folk art. When folks, even those who do not live in adorable villages or remote rural areas, put their abilities and imaginations toward the creation of something of use and beauty, *that* is folk art. We don't need a new Folk, we need a new definition.

One letter wanted to make certain that the book would contain nothing "kitschy." I'm not sure what that means exactly because one person's kitsch is another's couth. In my efforts not to be exclusionary, but rather to reflect the American-Jewish population—which is incredibly multifaceted—I may very well have included projects that are above or below some readers' sewing skills, Judaica knowledge, or aesthetic predilections. A Hasidic saying teaches us that "in everyone there is something precious, found in no one else, so honor each person for what is hidden within—for what they alone have, and none of their fellows." Or put slightly differently:

> All God's critters have a place in the choir,
> Some sing low and some sing higher.
> Some hum along on the telephone wire.
> Some just clap their hands.

The work included in this book represents the diversity of what is out there. It is meant to inspire you to pull out your fabric stash and make your own projects. That way, a few thousand years from now, the archaeologists will find many wonderful Judaic textiles representing our lives in this last decade of the twentieth century. I can think of no better way to close this Preface than the way I did in 1972, with these words from the 90th Psalm:

> Let the Graciousness of the Lord our God be upon us;
> Establish Thou also upon us the work of our hands;
> Yes, the work of our hands establish Thou it.

Tishri, 5753

PART ONE

Creating Heirlooms

heirloom *n* [ME *heirlome*, fr. *heir* + *lome* implement]
1: a piece of property that descends to the heir as an inseparable part of an inheritance   2: something of special value handed on from one generation to another.

Webster's New Collegiate Dictionary

Years ago, I gave my mother a cassette recorder for Mother's Day. She wanted, she said, to record memories of her childhood in Poland for me, memories that had given her the strength to live through the difficult times; the strength to come to America as a girl of sixteen never to see her parents again; the strength to endure the death of her two-year-old firstborn to pneumonia and not have the money for a tombstone because the Great Depression had taken away my father's picture-frame and glass store.

When I was cleaning out my mother's apartment after her death (my father having died the year before), I found the recorder and in it a cassette with the number "one" in my mother's handwriting. I put it on and after a silence full of breathing and rustling my father said, *"Oy, es is azoy heis heindt!"* (Wow, it's so hot today!) For the next five minutes I listened to my parents playing with the cassette recorder, figuring out how it worked, saying ordinary things self-consciously, and then agreeing to finish later. The rest of the cassette is blank and there are no others. Yet my mother left me a different kind of legacy of which she would have been proud.

I finally understand the message in my mother's death. When my first son, David, become a bar mitzvah, in the midst of all the joyousness, my mother said, "I am so happy to be at David's bar mitzvah celebration; I should only live to see Jeffrey's!" Come on, Ma," I reprimanded her. "Don't talk that way. In this country we wait for the Tooth Fairy, not the Angel of Death!" Two and a half years later, at Jeffrey's bar mitzvah celebration, my mother handed me a State of Israel Bond made out to Keren and said, "I should only live to Keren's bat mitzvah, but in case I don't make it, she should know I took care of her." And again I told her not to talk that way, that of course she would be there.

Six years later Keren became a bat mitzvah and my mother was there. It was a Reform shul in Brookline, Massachusetts, and so on that Shabbat morning my mother had the first *aliyah* in her life, when she was called upon to say the blessings for the Torah reading. I can see her now, on the *bimah* (platform) wearing boots because of the snow and a red turbanlike hat (which she apologized for but said she was accustomed to her Conservative synagogue where married women always cover their hair for services), saying the Torah blessings in her beautiful Yiddish-accented Hebrew. She walked around the *bimah* shaking everyone's hands like an old pro even though it was her first *aliyah* and her last.

As Shabbos came to a close and three stars appeared in the sky, my mother died. She made it through the service and the festive lunch. But as daylight left, taking with it her extra Shabbos soul, her frail heart stopped. When the emergency squad came and the sainted policeman George Finnegan gave her CPR and tried those black electric things to jolt her heart alive again, I could feel her soul

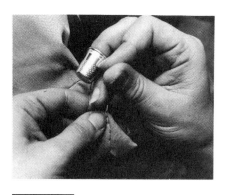

Figure 1-1

The work of our hands begins with a single stitch. *Photograph by Richard Speedy.*

hovering, saying to him, "Don't worry yourself, young man. It's all right; I did everything I had to do."

If she had been really vain, she would have stood up and shouted, "Hallelujah! I made it! I lived to Keren's bat mitzvah!" But she wasn't that theatrical. And with the shock and aftermath of her death I didn't really understand until recently that all those years when I thought my mother was being negative by saying, "I should only live until Keren's bat mitzvah," she was, in reality, psyching herself up to do just that. So, the most precious gift my mother left me was the message that I can do anything that I want badly enough.

Now that I have been elevated to "bubbie-hood," I often think about my mother's legacy and what I want to add to it.

I turned to make Judaica not only because it is tactilely and visually satisfying, but because it helps me to resolve a concrete spiritual problem. If I were a Hasid or an Israeli I would feel that every day my very existence was Jewish. I would live by the Jewish calendar, instead of dipping into it primarily for holidays. I'd speak and read Hebrew, instead of or along with English. But, like most American Jews, I live a hyphenated life. I am not making apologies. I find it exhilarating and satisfying to be part of an open pluralistic society. But I need to manifest my Jewishness; and since making my first *hallah* cover as a bride of eighteen while living in Ishiki Hayama, a Japanese village outside the U.S. Naval Base at Yokosuka, I found that creating something Jewish, using all of my best skills, nourishes and calms my soul.

Now I want to make a pile of "things of special value," heirlooms, if you will, to give to my children and grandchildren. Even more important, I want to inspire and teach them and you how to make your own heirlooms. You will know it is an heirloom if every time you handle the treasured object it vibrates with meaning and with memories.

The Creative Process and Developing a Personal Style

"Wait a minute," you say. "You are talking about vibrating heirlooms and I can't even draw." I hear that often. Many of us are intimidated about drawing because we mistakenly believe that all drawings are meant to look a certain way. Then, when we compare our work and it doesn't look conventional or ordinary, or like something we have already seen somewhere (even though we are ready to admire innovation in others), we assume that we have failed. The *news* is that drawing, designing, and stitching are autographic. Everyone's work is as individual as a fingerprint.

I wish I could tell you that designing is easy; that design is endlessly creative and spontaneous; that trials do not lead to error. But it isn't so. Design, like life, is difficult but not impossible. Once you recognize this you can relax and enjoy yourself. The single most important factor in creating a successful design is neither technical skill nor the ability to draw but simply self-confidence.

Self-confidence is blostered by the genuine desire to create something personal and unique and by quantities of persistence. Don't panic; trust yourself. If you think you can't draw, trace designs, patching together bits and pieces of images you like. Use that wonderful gift of technology, the copy machine, to enlarge, reduce, and make multiples of your image. Cut and tear paper shapes; use photographs. In short do *anything* to get started. When you find a motif or design that pleases you, use it over and over again in different sizes, colors, and combinations. Don't be afraid to copy. When you borrow from other sources it is called research. When you develop a good design and repeat it and interpret it in various techniques and materials, it is called "style." (Of course, when you borrow from one source for purposes of fame or gain, *that* is called plagiarism.)

Researching and Interpreting Authentic Jewish Symbols and Motifs

Although my home is in the heart of Jewish Boston, and I am within walking distance of at least seven sources of fresh bagels and hallah and at least that many synagogues, I am always aware that I live in the greater diaspora. By being even the least bit involved in the general community's life, where more than sixty different languages are spoken, I have been fortunate to become friends with people from a wide range of backgrounds. Over the cookies at a political coffee or the zinnia beds at the neighborhood landscape effort we ask one another what we do in "real life." When I tell folks, even Jewish ones, that I make and write about Jewish needlecraft or textile art, they look confused and then blurt out something like, "What's Jewish about sewing? How is Jewish sewing different from 'normal' sewing?" After many backyard discussions I have finally figured out how to describe what it is that I do. It isn't the sewing per se, I explain; any technique will do. It is what we make and how we embellish it that makes it Jewish.

What makes an object or a symbol Jewish, however, is sometimes almost as thorny a question as what makes a person Jewish. Just as holidays change their meanings and observances over time, so too are symbols and motifs interpreted differently in different times and places. To the bafflement of researchers documenting the decorations of ancient synagogues in northern Israel, the symbols used most often were not the *esrog, lulav,* and *menorah,* which they expected to find, but rather the Roman eagle fighting a snake. They didn't understand the

Figure 1-2
Detail from drawing "When Moses Got to Heaven He Found the Angels Weaving
the Alef-Bet into a Crown for God," by Myron Tupa.

meaning it had for the Jews of the period. Perhaps, they thought, it was
a way of rendering unto Caesar what was felt to be due unto Caesar—a
form of political recognition, much as Jews in America today use the
flag and Statue of Liberty to reflect a spirit of nationalism. We can't
know with any certainty.

In this century we have seen the swastika transformed from an
innocuous sun symbol for happiness into the emblem of absolute evil
and destruction. Some scholars say that the swastika orginated with
the ancient Hebrews, who used it as a sign for the flaming swords of
the cherubim who protected the Garden of Eden after Adam and Eve
were expelled (Gen. 3:24). It will be centuries, if ever, before this
ancient good-luck charm can redeem itself from the horror it inspires.

Many motifs and symbols used in Jewish life have lost favor
because they were adopted by the surrounding non-Jewish culture.
For example, this is what happened (and is still happening) to the
symbol of the wreath. We know from the Hanukkah story that when
Judah and his men recaptured the Temple they cleaned and

Figure 1-3

Postcard from 1911 showing the swastika as a symbol of love, life, light, and good luck.

refurbished it in order to rededicate it. According to the first book of Maccabees they "decked the front of the Temple with crowns of gold and small shields." Crowns in that period were wreaths.

Another example is that Hanukkah was originally celebrated as a second Sukkot to make up for the one that went unobserved while the battle for the liberation of the Temple raged. In that era part of the Sukkot observance called for wearing leafy wreaths. It was, after all, a harvest festival. Because the use of wreaths was so prevalent in Jewish observance during the fourth century C.E., an early church leader issued a warning to Christians to avoid the use of wreaths, because it was "the custom of Greeks and Jews." Apparently the Christians paid little attention to this injunction, and today we see wreaths not only used as a quasireligious folk symbol during Christmas but also made from many materials and used throughout the year. The Hanukkah wreath, like the Hanukkah bush, just hasn't made it. The crown continues to be used by Jews as a symbol, but the meaning has changed from a military victory crown to that of the crown of the majesty of the Law.

As fashions changed, the wreath/crown was replaced with the more hatlike crown we associate with Jewish decoration. Torah scrolls in the synagogue are often adorned with finely crafted crowns. Rabbi Simeon ben Yohai, in the second century, said, "There are three crowns, the crown of learning, the crown of priesthood, and the crown of royalty; but the crown of a good name excels them all" (*Pirke Avot* IV, 17). A good example of this theme is the Halpern family of *mizrah*, designed by Alice Nussbaum and worked by Noreen Halpern (Part Three, Fig. 3-6).

Swastikas are unthinkable; wreaths, especially those in red and green, are basically unusable; but what about angels? Can we use angels in Jewish art and decoration? Why not? Some say that because angels and cherubim have been so widely used in church decoration they are off limits for Jewish embellishment. Similarly, because the heart has been used so much in Catholicism we can't use it either. The same goes for fishes. I am ready to discard the swastika and to let the wreath rest, but I am not prepared to give up hearts, fishes, and angels! Angels have a long and complex Jewish pedigree. It is said that when Moses got to heaven he found the angels weaving the alef-bet into a crown for God. Now isn't that a great combination of images and a good enough reason for using them in our designs?

It is all a matter of interpretation. Judaism is an orthopraxy rather than an orthodoxy. This means that even in the symbols we choose, it's what they do and what we do with them that counts. There is a thin line between religion and superstition, between nostalgia and belief. In order to use authentic Jewish motifs in our design work we must arm ourselves with research and study. As we dip into history, hoping for inspiration, we need to have a bit of patience and to think through and feel what the symbols and stories we are contemplating mean for Jews in our day and age. It takes homework, even legwork, and a few sharp pencils. Remember, we are talking about heirlooms here, not "kwik" decorations made out of aluminum foil and paper plates.

Immerse yourself in your subject. The more you read and look, the more symbols will be available to you and the more ideas you will have. Keep your eyes open for images you are interested in portraying. Food advertisements, for example, are great sources for pictures of biblical fruits and vegetables. Colors you like and naturally gravitate to are the colors to use. If you get nervous about picking colors, look at the colors of your clothes, or those of the room around you, and you will see that you've already made many selections. Use what you like and are most familiar with. Once you have something you like, repeat it over and over again; it will change every time you use it and eventually you will have developed your own style. Remember what we said earlier: style comes from repeating yourself. If there is a shape you particularly like, a *menorah* perhaps, repeat it to build a pattern. Repetition is the skeleton of a design; variation is its intelligence. If you have made a checkerboard using your stylized *menorah* design in black and white, for example, consider having one in red to add that spark of intellect.

We know that the *menorah*, the seven-branched lamp, is the oldest Jewish symbol continuously used in two, if not three, dimensions. The Star of David, which today is most commonly associated with Jews and Jewish life, is in fact a new symbol. The color combination of sky blue and white is often thought of as *the* Jewish colors and indeed they have been for very long time, but scarlet, purple, and blue used with linen is an even older combination going back to the desert tabernacle (Exod. 25:8).

Figure 1-4
"*Menorah* with Happy Lions and Doves" (single-fold). The seven-branched *menorah* is recognized as the oldest Jewish symbol and is now the emblem of the State of Israel. See the "Strong as a Lion" *parokhet* (ark curtain) in Color Plate 2.

The Talmud, quoting Abaye, says *"Simana milta hi"* (Signs are meaningful). Try your hand at these and other lesser-known themes and signs. Study, research, and practice in order to learn new interpretations and to invest the objects you make with the value of time lovingly spent. Here is a brief list to start you off:

Bells	Candles	Doves
Elephants	Behemoth	Leviathan
Winged Creatures	Seven Species	Pillars
Snakes	Lamed-Vavniks	Ark

Throughout this book you will find objects, symbols, and motifs that resonate with Jewish meaning. Many of them are in pattern or silhouette form in order to make it easier for you to jump off into a project of your own. Other work is shown here to introduce source material from which you can draw further information and inspiration.

The Alef-Bet: The Consummate Jewish Symbol

The twenty-two-letter Hebrew alef-bet derives from the same ancient Phoenician letters as does the Roman alphabet used for English and other European languages. By looking closely you can see their common heredity. Because Hebrew is written from right to left and the Roman alphabet from left to right, the letters often appear as mirror images of the same basic form. Another characteristic that makes them appear to differ more than they really do is the emphasis placed on the vertical line in the Roman alphabet and on the characteristic horizontal stroke in the Hebrew.

With some variations in vowel usage the Hebrew alef-bet is also used for *Judezmo* (Ladino, based on the Castillian Spanish of preexpulsion Spain) and Yiddish, which has been used by Ashkenazic Jews for the last 1,000 years and is based on medieval German with an admixture of Hebrew and the local language of the particular diaspora where it was being spoken. Hebrew letters have also been used to write Arabic and Turkish by the Karaite Jews in the Crimea. All twenty-two of the Hebrew letters are consonants. Vowel sounds are

Figure 1-5
"Crowned Alef," laid and couched embroidery. Photograph by Dennis Gallaway.

Figure 1-6
The letters *gimel*, *resh*, and *fe* with their Roman alphabet mirror images.

indicated by the use of six signs made of lines and dots placed below, above, or in the center of the letter. The vowel signs are not used in the Torah scroll or contemporary newspapers but rather mainly for teaching Hebrew. Five of the letters have a different form when used at the end of the word:

כך ,מם ,נן ,פף ,צץ

Five variants are created by placing a dot inside or above the letter.

בב ,כך ,פף ,שׁשׂ ,תּת

Square, or block, Hebrew is used for most printing, whether by hand for ceremonial articles or mechanically for newspapers and posters. Hebrew cursive is used primarily for letters, notes, business, and legal documents. Because it is less formal, less imbued with sanctity, and very curvilinear, it can be extremely decorative in the right project. Basically the same for thousands of years, the alef-bet has taken on various styles in different locations and eras. A good source for different lettering styles and sizes is rub-off transfer letters, which can be found in the graphics or stationery department of a large Jewish bookstore. Stencils, which are useful for familiarizing yourself with the basic form of the letters, are also available.

This is not the place for a complete treatise on Hebrew language, grammar, or even calligraphy. There are, however, a number of points I would like to cover in order to help you avoid pitfalls that might cause you to distort a letter or phrase beyond recognition.

When transliterating English or other foreign names or words in Hebrew, you will need sounds not ordinarily used. The following system has been devised for putting foreign words into Hebrew characters:

When a vowel is needed, use *alef* for A.
Use *alef* + *yod* for I and E at the beginning of words.
Use *yod* for Y when it sounds like the Y in "yes" and for E and U in the middle of a word.
Use *vav* for O in the middle of a word and *alef* + *vav* for O at the beginning of a word.
There is no J sound (as in Jessica) or Ch (as in Charles) in Hebrew, so the practice has developed of using accented letters for these sounds. The J is indicated by a *gimel* with an accent mark over it, and the Ch with a similarly accented *tzadi*.
W, as in Wendy, is indicated with two *vavim*.
Tav is used for Th, as in Theodore.

Using Hebrew letters for transliteration has given rise to many cross-lingual misspellings. Remember, too, that Hebrew reads from right to left!

Now that we have discussed the basics of the alef-bet itself, we

THE HEBREW ALEF-BET

Letter	Name	Sound	Value	Script
א	Alef	Silent	1	
בּ	Bet	B	2	
ב	Vet	V	2	
ג	Gimel	G (get)	3	
ד	Dalet	D	4	
ה	Hay	H	5	
ו	Vav	V	6	
ז	Zayin	Z	7	
ח	Het	CH (challah)	8	
ט	Tet	T	9	
י	Yod	Y	10	
כּ	Kaf	K	20	
כ	Chaf	CH (challah)		
ך	Final Chaf			
ל	Lamed	L	30	
מ	Mem	M	40	
ם	Final Mem			
נ	Nun	N	50	
ן	Final Nun			
ס	Samekh	S	60	
ע	Ayin	Silent	70	
פּ	Pe	P	80	
פ	Fe	F		
ף	Final Fe			
צ	Tzadi	TZ	90	
ץ	Final Tzadi			
ק	Kof	K	100	
ר	Resh	R	200	
שׁ	Shin	SH	300	
שׂ	Sin	S		
ת	Tav	T	400	

Figure 1-7
Table of the alef-bet.

come to some design issues. Although lettering on labels and dedications needs to be clearly legible, often this very quality will be counterproductive and boring in design work. Adding a Hebrew word or two certainly identifies an object as Jewish, but unless the letters themselves form part of the design and are visually integrated into the

אבגדהוזחטי

יכלמםננס ע

פןצ צקרשת

Figure 1-8
Basic block form of the alef-bet.

other elements of the composition, they may very well detract from its overall meaning and beauty. The eye will tend to read the words rather than respond to the entire design unless care and artistry have been employed. The style of the alef-bet chosen, and the sizes and placement of the letters, should be determined as much by the size and shape of the object in question as by the literal meaning of the message. With care, letters can be manipulated to fill the special requirements of your project.

There are no capital letters in Hebrew. Instead, when emphasis at the beginning of a paragraph is desired, the entire first word is often enlarged and embellished and treated as a decorative panel. Syllables are traditionally not divided in Hebrew. In order to make all lines equal and have even margins on the page, six letters can be expanded horizontally. These are *dalet*, *hay*, *het*, *lamed*, *tav*, and *resh*.

The negative space—what is left out—is as important visually as

Figure 1-9
Calligraphy by David Moss showing enlarged initial word and expanded letters.

the positive elements of the design. Because all the letters are not the same width, and in order to avoid gaps or crowding, it is a good idea to keep round letters such as *pe* or *samekh* fairly close to their neighbors, but to leave more space between letters with long verticals, such as *hay*, *tav*, and *vav*.

When you are in the planning stage, remember to leave space for the ascending line of the *lamed* and the dropped verticals of the *kof* and the final *nun*, *khaf*, *pe*, and *tzadi*. You can do this by leaving the space between the lines as wide as a letter is high. Another, more enjoyable, way—which takes more preplanning—is to juggle the lines a bit so that the long verticals fit into empty spaces left in the preceding line by letters such as *yod*, *resh*, and *dalet*.

Just as there is a huge difference in sound, usage, and meaning between the letters "O" and "Q" in the Roman alphabet, in Hebrew also what appears to be a minute difference can completely change a letter.

Once you are certain of the letters you want to use, try cutting them out of paper and moving them around on a background the size of the object you plan to make. You may discover that in order to properly fill a space you have to extend a line or thicken a curve. In

Figure 1-10
Cursive alef-bet.

Figure 1-11

The name David; playing with the letters to incorporate royal and musical associations.

Figure 1-12

Jessica's first sampler, 1992.

Figure 1-13

Jessica's modified cross-stitch alef-bet.

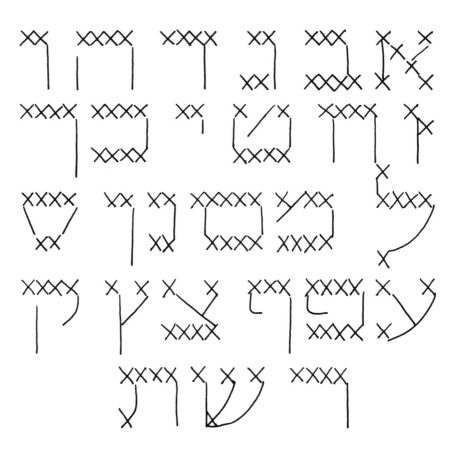

that case, cut a new pattern piece or tape an additional piece of paper to your original letter. With patience and practice come familiarity. The letters and symbols will eventually work together visually to produce a pleasing whole.

Legend tells us that God especially loved the *alef* for its humility. It is always silent, taking its identify from those around it. So God rewarded the *alef* by giving it first place in the *alef-bet* and first place in the Decalogue. As you work with these letters, you too may develop favorites. A single word or letter can be turned into an intriguing design. You might even plan an entire project around a single letter by repeating it to form a pattern. For example, try playing with the letters in your name to invent your own personal logo.

The two alfa-bets shown in Figs. 1-13 and 1-14 were designed for my granddaughters, Jessica, who was five and learning how to cross-stitch, and Alana, who was seven and a more experienced sewer. Alana was ready to do her sampler using the conventional cross-stitch alef-bet. It had too many x's for Jessica and proved daunting. The modified alef-bet we created for her allows for greater freedom in the linear stitches, which can be chain, outline, or running stitches.

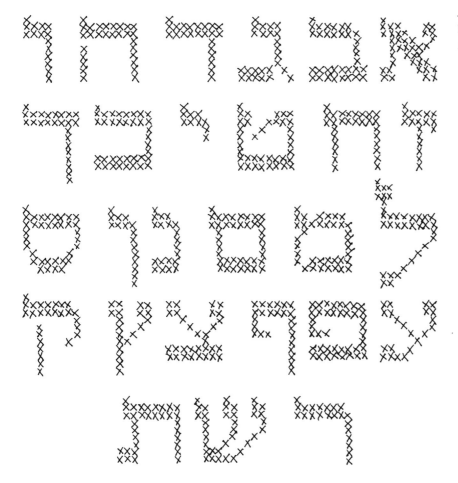

Figure 1-14
Alana's basic cross-stitch alef-bet.

Figure 1-15

Traditional alef-bet; 2½″ high, for appliqué and embroidery. Use the *fe sofit* without center element for the final *chaf*.

Figure 1-15
continued

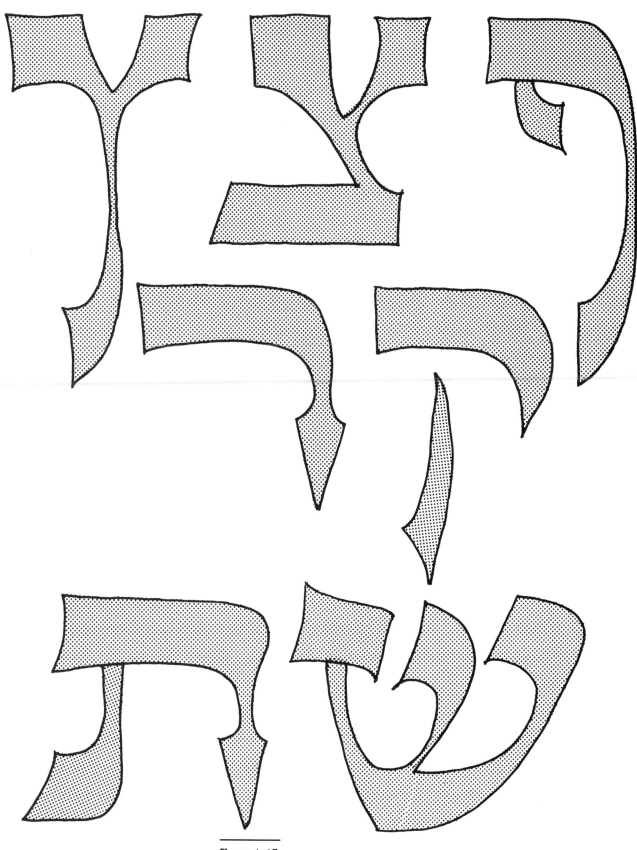

Figure 1-15
continued

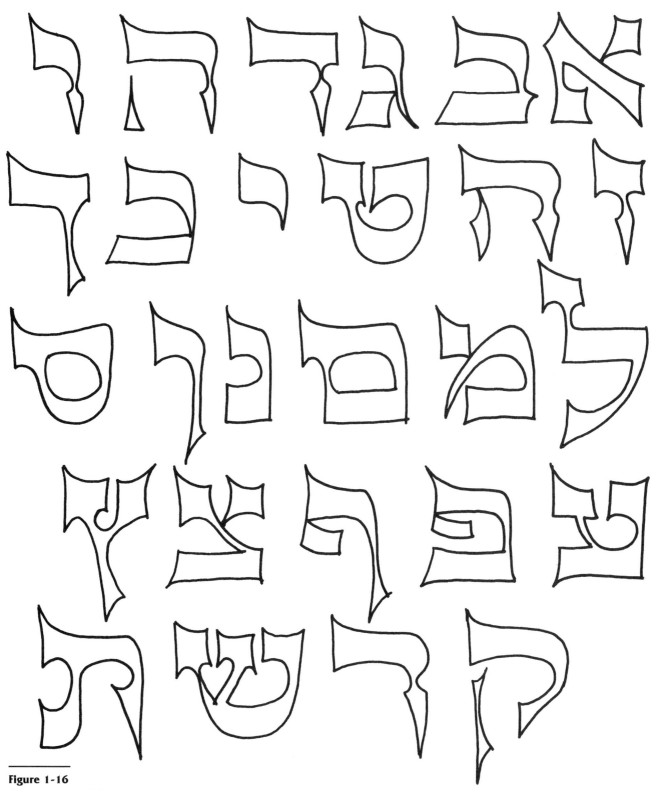

Figure 1-16
Contemporary alef-bet.

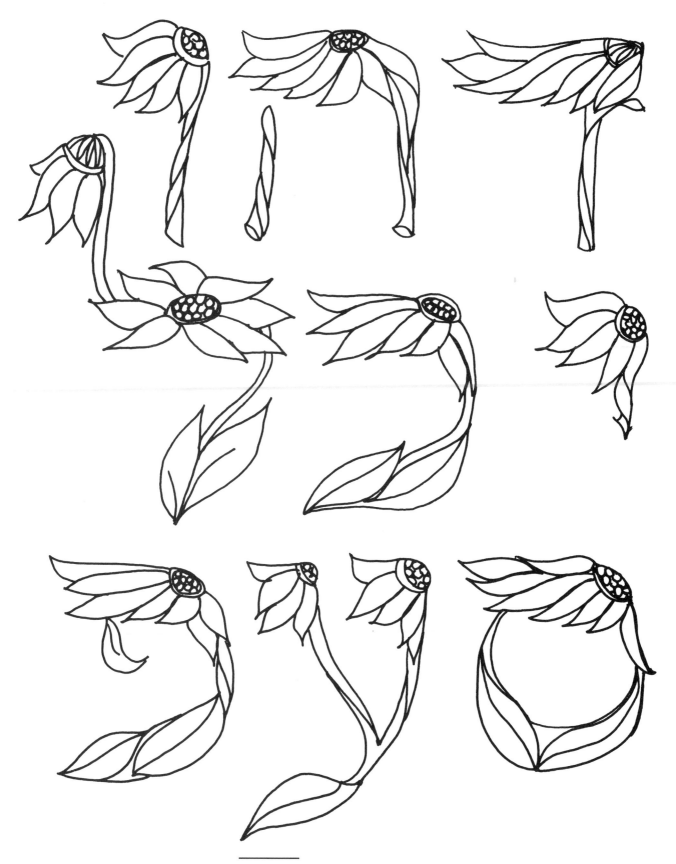

Figure 1-17
Flower alef-bet; use *fe sofit* without center leaf for final *chaf*.

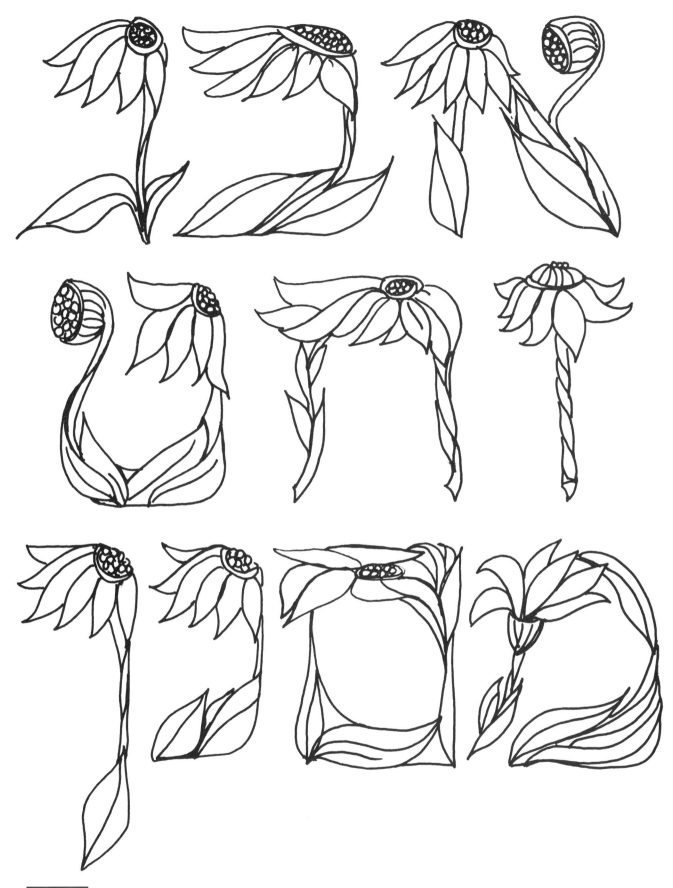

Figure 1-17
continued

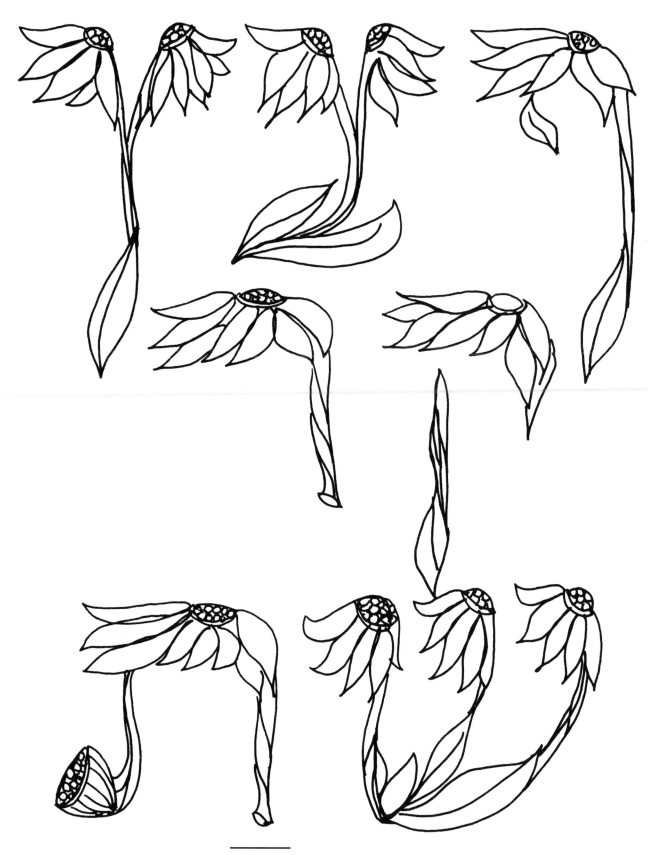

Figure 1-17
continued

Planning and Using Paper-cuts as a Design Tool

I didn't get my driver's license until I was thirty-seven, earning that precious document just twenty minutes before my son David, who got his license on his seventeenth birthday. I am learning how to use a computer as I write this book.

My timing was better with other skills. I grew up bilingual, with Yiddish as my *mama loshen* (mother tongue) and English as my second

Figure 1-18
Nineteenth- or early twentieth-century Moravian paper-cut *mizrah* with watercolor decoration.

language. A happy by-product of living in Yiddish as a child is that I learned the Hebrew alef-bet, both square and script, for reading and writing when I was very young and I learned how to make paper-cuts at my mother's knee in that Bronx kitchen where my heart returns at the beginning of almost every project. Over the years paper-cutting techniques and stylized imagery have served me well for many types of artwork from serigraphy to quilts.

If you live long enough you get a chance to try (and perhaps do) just about everything. Maybe not in the usual order, but that doesn't matter. If you are a little timid about trying paper-cutting, jump in anyway. This may be the perfect time for *you*, and just the technique you were searching for to help plan your next textile project. Or it may turn out to be the perfect medium to express some previously trapped ideas.

Although decorations have been cut from bark, parchment, fabric, and paper for thousands of years all over the world, it is believed that paper-cutting as we know it was brought to Europe from China by Marco Polo. Just as every cultural group uses variants of the same universal crafts to create things that satisfy both its physical and spiritual needs, Jewish artists have at one time or another worked at

Figure 1-19
Roysalah, quadruple-fold paper-cut.

just about every craft imaginable. For the past few centuries paper-cutting has been a popular folk craft.

The nineteenth- and early-twentieth-century Jews of Eastern Europe made paper-cuts as *mizrahim* (ornaments for the eastern wall of the home), *shivvitim* (votive wall decorations), amulets (particularly for new mothers). Simhat Torah flags, and round flower-shaped window decorations for Shavuot called *roysalakh* (little roses). These paper-cuts were as fragile as the people; few examples survived the Second World War.

Our concern here is not to make art paper-cuts on "good" paper to be preserved and framed. Instead we will discuss the basic tools and techniques of paper-cutting and how to use your paper-cuts to plan your textile projects.

Use strong, thin paper. Most typing paper is excellent as are some brands of shelf and freezer paper. Newsprint isn't strong enough and construction paper is a bit heavy and coarse, but if you are doing a single-fold design it is workable.

Assemble tools for cutting. My mother said that the men in the village (whose efforts at this craft were, of course, taken more seriously) tacked the folded paper to a board and cut out the design with a knife. Women and girls made paper-cuts with scissors much as Polish

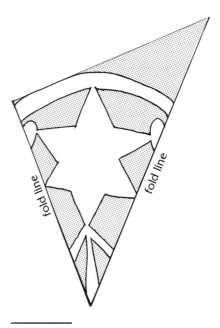

Figure 1-20
Pattern for paper-cut in Fig. 1-19. Cut away the shaded areas.

Figure 1-21
"Passover" (double-fold). Four cups of wine, four children, and four questions.

and German women do *scherenschnitte*. I use both methods and for some cuts even combine them. My favorite tool, the No. 11 X-Acto hobby knife, is as easy to use as a pencil. Sharp 5″ scissors, embroidery and/or cuticle scissors, and pinking shears all come in handy. Do not use your sewing scissors; cutting paper is guaranteed to dull the blades and sometimes pop the screw.

For your first paper-cuts choose symbols that are easily shown in silhouette. A crown, birds, the Star of David, the tablets, a goblet—all are simple to draw or trace. When you are more expert, progress to elaborately intertwined foliage, beasts, and thematic material. If you have not done this before, expect to be pleasantly surprised at how elaborate the simplest drawing becomes when it is transformed into a multiple image.

Fold the paper in half, fourths, sixths, or, as in the case with the *roysalah* shown in Fig. 1-19, in eighths. This is done by folding a square piece of paper in half, over on itself into quarters, and then in half diagonally from corner to center into eighths. Though they appear complicated, the most pizzazz for the least amount of drawing is achieved with this quadruple-fold cut, which will give you eight repeats for one drawing. Before beginning to draw you might want to even up the edges of the folded sheet.

Figure 1-22
"Shabbat" (single-fold). The rays, which hold the paper-cut together, will be embroidered lines on my appliqué.

Although the quadruple-fold is easy to draw, it is cumbersome to cut. For your very first paper-cut you might be happier trying a double-fold, which divides the paper in fourths, giving you four repeats. A single-fold will produce a double mirror image. Study the paper-cuts shown here and their accompanying drawings to help you decide where and how to start your own. A nonfolded paper-cut is the most difficult because the drawing and the composition needs to be well thought out beforehand and carefully done.

Draw your design lightly on the folded paper. Remember, you only need to draw the design once; the folding will provide the repeats. Clearly delineate each shape; that is, don't sketch and shade but instead do a hard-edge cartoon. Make certain that each shape touches a neighboring form just enough, but no more, to keep it from falling apart as you begin cutting. If you want a central image, a *menorah*, for example, draw only half of it along the central fold line. Pay attention to the direction your motifs are facing. If your birds are looking at a fold line, they will be looking at one another when the cut is opened. Paper-cuts lend themselves well to distortion, so feel free to manipulate the shapes to fill the space. Small geometric shapes, scrolls, and foliage can be used to tie your symbols together.

Using your sharpest, pointiest scissors or utility knife, cut details,

Figure 1-23
"Adam and Eve" (single-fold). After the basic shapes are cut out, open the paper to add definition to the figures and the snake.

Figure 1-24
"Rosh Hashanah."

Figure 1-25
"Simhat Torah." The first and last letters of the Torah were used to suggest
the continuity of the Torah reading cy-
cle.

Figure 1-26
Stencil form alef-bet.

Figure 1-27
"Hanukkah" (single-fold).

Figure 1-28
"Jacob's Ladder" (diagonal single-fold).

such as the eye of a bird, first. It is easier to be precise while there is more paper to hold onto. Then cut away the background paper. If you find yourself cutting where you didn't intend to, use some tape for the time being; then, next time, before beginning to cut, quickly shade or otherwise mark the negative spaces that will be cut away.

If letters are part of your design, unfold the paper and draw them *lightly* on the front of the paper-cut. Then proceed with the cutting. Most of the letters present little or no problem for paper-cut use. Some, however, have hollow centers that fall out when you cut the outline away. In order to have a unified alef-bet for paper-cuts, I developed the stencil-form letters shown in Fig. 1-26. When the cutting is finished to your satisfaction, unfold carefully and gently press with a warm iron to remove the fold marks.

The paper-cuts shown here are square because each one is being used as a pattern for appliqué quilt patches for a Baltimore Album (Judaic-style) quilt I am working on. The different elements will be done in a variety of fabrics and embroidered details will embellish each square. The Jacob's Ladder pattern with the two angels in Fig.

Figure 1-29
"And Grant Thee Peace," paper-cut.

1-28 is being worked as an embroidered *hallah* cover to illustrate the popular Sabbath song, "*Shalom Alaykhem*," which welcomes the "angels most high" to the Sabbath table.

Lynne Lederman, a member of the Greater Boston Chapter of the Pomegranate Guild of Judaic Needlework (more about this organization in Part Three), who has been designing and making a wide variety of synagogue textiles, brought to one of our meetings a charming crib-size quilt she made based on the designs shown here (see Color Plate 1). Lynne copied Xeroxes of the designs onto plastic film to use as opaque transparencies (negatives) for the blueprints. She then placed the transparencies over pieces of bleached cotton muslin that had been treated with chemicals similar to those used for architect's blueprints. The fabric was exposed to sunlight and then washed to develop them. The quilt was assembled and pieced by machine, using a rich blue cotton madras print for the sashing, and then quilted by hand with light blue thread.

Use these paper-cuts as departure points to devise your own if you like and then go on to use them for your needlework. You can trace around the various motifs for embroidery or use them as patterns for appliqué. The visual tension created in a paper-cut by having all the

Figure 1-30
Silkscreen printed fabric drying in my old studio. *Photograph by Richard Speedy.*

elements touch can sometimes feel crowded when translated to textile work. Unless you are totally enamored with the finished paper-cut, you might want to separate the various motifs and play with them on a larger sheet of contrasting background paper to see if they form an even better design. As you read this book you will see many of the symbols shown here worked in different ways.

A number of years ago, the Pratt Graphic Art Center in New York City announced an invitational exhibition called "The Printed Quilt; The Quilted Print." Because I was actively involved in printmaking at that time, I accepted the invitation and also decided that my quilted print-quilt would have a Judaic theme. Having recently completed a series of etchings and screenprints with the theme of Jewish

Figure 1-31
"And Grant Thee Peace," 96″ × 108″. This quilt traveled around the country for more than two years with an exhibit sponsored by the Pratt Graphic Art Center.

mysticism, I decided that my quilt would be a "protective" amulet quilt, keeping guard "against the evil eye." My first step was to make a paper-cut with the symbols and Hebrew phrase (And Grant Thee Peace) I wanted to use (Fig. 1-29). Using textile inks I then printed enough fabric in a variety of colors for a double-bed-size quilt. After the fabric was printed, I cut it apart and then reassembled the image in three different colors. When the quilt was fully assembled and bordered, a number of friends helped me set up a full-size quilting frame and we quilted it in several sessions (see Color Plate 3).

Two last words about heirlooms: sign them! Any of the alphabets here can be used for your signature. Remember that they can all be photographically reduced (or enlarged). The basic linear ones in Figs. 1-8 and 1-10 work well for long inscriptions. Or you might prefer to invent a logo for yourself. Be kind to your heirs and the archaeologists: add the date. Depending on how it fits into the piece, I will use some variation of my Hebrew and English first name, along with the year, on all of my future Judaica work.

Figure 1-32
My own personal "logo."

PART TWO

The Past

Long ago and far away there lived a man who, tiring of his village, decided to go to the big city in search of adventure. One morning he set off down the road leaving his wife and children bewildered in the doorway.

When night came he slept under a tree at the side of the

Figure 2-1
"God Made Man Because He Loves Stories," silkscreen print.

road. To make certain that he would not lose his way in the morning, he took off his boots and carefully pointed them in the direction of the big city. While he slept someone turned his boots around. In the morning our unsuspecting friend put on his boots and proceeded down the road in the direction they were now pointing. When the rooftops of the "city" appeared over the hillside they were surprisingly familiar. Entering the city gates and wandering down the streets it seemed the city was but a reflection of his village. From a doorway a child with eyes like his own called, "Please stay, please stay." The child was beautiful and the desire to rest after his travels was great so he remained in the city and never returned to his village.

Adapted from a Russian Folk Tale

God Made Man because He Loves Stories

The story of the Jews has been a circling tale of clinging to eternal beliefs and values while adjusting and adapting to new life-styles in countries around the world.

Jewish textiles for decorative and ritual purposes date back to the earliest period of recorded history. The Holy Scriptures contain specific instructions for making the textiles for the Tabernacle in the desert and for priestly garments. Many extant examples of embroidered, woven, and sewn artifacts from both the European and Eastern Jewish communities document the importance of the fiber arts in ancient as well as modern times. As the Jews have wandered, their artwork, as their lives, has taken on the style of those they lived among. In textiles, therefore, as in life, it is *what* is made that has been and is important, rather than a particular style or technique.

For this chapter, we draw our inspiration from the Bible and legend, from the broad spread of Jewish history that spans millenia and geography, and from American needlework traditions.

Projects: Torah, Legend, History

Bereshit (Gen.), the appliqué wall hanging depicting Adam and Eve with the Snake, was made for Rabbi Harry Baum in New York City. Bright-colored cotton fabrics were strip-pieced to make up the patchwork snake, border, and letters. The faces of Adam and Eve were drawn with pen and ink. The *menorah*-form tree partially screens a crown with a large eye, which is meant to signify the all-seeing Holy One. The figures were appliquéd to a navy blue woolen background using an enlarged blind stitch and bright-colored #5 and #3 cotton pearl thread (see Color Plate 4).

Miriam K. Sokoloff does not consider herself an artist but rather a sewing teacher. Nevertheless, through educated and inspired research, careful interpretation, and meticulous craftsmanship, she energetically creates a stream of marvelous Judaic textiles. Miriam began sewing at the age of five and using the sewing machine at seven. Since 1981 she has been a prolific quiltmaker, with most of her work having Judaic themes. The vest in Fig. 2-2 is based on a stained glass medallion her mother, Deborah S. Kandler, made, depicting the biblical Miriam dancing with cymbals. The design, which has become her logo, was used as the cover for Miriam's bat mitzvah invitation and now appears on her letterhead. While sewing the vest Miriam was also working on the "stained glass" appliqués described in Part Three (see Fig. 3-39). These were too big to carry around, so Miriam used the

Figure 2-2
"Miriam's Vest," stained glass appliqué by Miriam K. Sokoloff.

same techniques to make her vest, which was portable and could easily be brought to meetings and waiting rooms.

"Stained glass" appliqué is a technique similar to mola and reverse appliqué. It was popularized in the April 1978 edition of *Quilter's Newsletter Magazine*, which featured a quilt made by the students of the technique's originator, California quilter Roberta Horton. Simply stated, the process imitates the effect of stained glass by sewing the desired shapes of pastel and jewel-toned fabric, arranging them to form a flat motif onto a light background cloth, and then outlining the design elements with double-fold black bias tape, which is carefully hand stitched in place. When well done, the effect is marvelous.

Miriam's wall quilt "Moses" (Color Plate 5) was inspired by a set

Figure 2-3

"When Moses Got to Heaven He Found the Angels Weaving the Letters of the Alef-Bet into a Crown for God." This drawing, by Myron Tupa, can be enlarged to any size you want and done in needlepoint or linear embroidery.

of Israeli stamps issued in August 1981. She came upon them while she was working on a pair of Log Cabin quilts for her daughters. She said that "the waves in the third stamp just jumped out and said, 'Quilt me.' " After deciding on the finished size, she enlarged the stamps by making a slide and projecting it onto large white paper taped to the wall. By adjusting the projector she was able to see the image of the size she wanted it to be. Using a sharp tracing wheel, Miriam cut cardboard templates of the major shapes. Each "stamp" was hand appliquéd and then joined with the others by machine-sewn sashing. The wall hanging was then hand quilted.

My husband, Myron Tupa, teacher of animation, cartooning, and printmaking, grew up making pictures and airplane models and using any tools or materials that came to hand. When he was eleven, his mother taught him to sew. Both Myron and I are intrigued by angels and angel lore and use Metatron, the angle in charge of the heavenly library and human sustenance (among his/her other chores), as the logo for our design studio.

A Hasidic saying tells us: "The virtue of angels is that they cannot deteriorate; their flaw is that they cannot improve. Man's flaw is that he can deteriorate; and his virtue is that he can improve." When I came across the *midrash* describing Moses reaching heaven to find the angels busy weaving the letters of the alef-bet into a crown for God, I asked Myron to draw it for me for my birthday. His rendition of the story makes my heart sing and was a natural to include in this book. So I asked him to embroider it for my next birthday. As an artist he approached this project with the same intensity as any other art project: shopping for days until he found the pink-mauve moiré for the sky, cutting the clouds across the grain so that they would reflect the

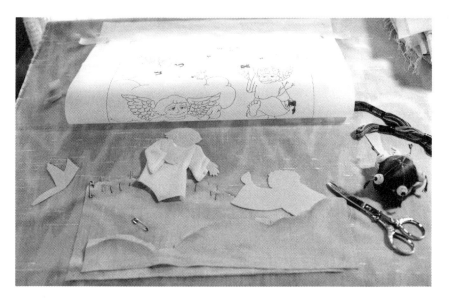

Figure 2-4
"Angels Weaving . . . ," appliqué in progress.

Figure 2-5
Detail, angel coming in for a landing with letters.

Figure 2-6
"In Memory of Sonja," handwoven silk *tallit* (prayer shawl) by Dini Moes. *Photograph courtesy of the artist.*

light differently when they were appliquéd in place, and combining single embroidery threads of different colors for the angels' hair. Their clothes are prewashed muslin carefully cut and draped. The faces, hands, and letters are broadcloth and cotton moiré that has been fused to an iron-on facing (see Color Plate 6 for finished piece).

The size of the piece was determined beforehand by a yard-sale frame that was waiting in our basement for years for the perfect piece to suggest itself. We bought it because of the pillars, intending one day to use it to frame a *mizrah* (an ornamental plaque for the eastern wall).

The drawings can be enlarged or reduced to any size you want, and the angels, letters, and clouds can be rearranged. Work the design in needlepoint, cross-stitch, appliqué, or linear embroidery. Enjoy! (Please send pictures.)

Themes from our collective, spiritual, or personal past can be interpreted and rendered in many ways. Andy Warhol said that "imagination cannot be copied, but it can be transferred from person to person and place to place." And, I would submit, from time to time.

California artist Peachy Levy writes that every time she starts a project she searches "for themes in the Torah, *midrash*, or other biblical writings that relate to the *mitzvah* associated with the ritual object. . . . I try to connect my contemporary Jewish experience with eternal Jewish values." As you study her Torah mantles (Color Plate 7) you will see her abstract interpretation of a crowned Tree of Life with the words "From generation to generation" below; a *menorah* with gold sparks at the top showing that we are enlightened by Torah; and Tablets of the law floating over land and water with the quotation "one Law for all time for your generations." On the top row is the Torah dedicated to the Holocaust. For this very difficult theme Peachy used the burning bush to represent the survivors, the *menorah* to identify Israel, and Moses' response to God—"*Hineni*" ("Here I am")—as the Jewish peoples' collective response to those nightmare years.

Weaver Dini Moes made the silk tallit in Fig. 2-6 as well as a companion *tallit* bag in memory of her friend Sonja. The design of stripes in seven shades of blue (seven times a day do I praise Thee) is based on the prayer "May the tallit spread its wings over them and save them."

Dini writes: "We were in the same schools and colleges together in Amsterdam, The Netherlands. When we parted in 1942, we said we would see each other later, but this was not to be. . . . I am not of the Jewish faith, but a friend is a friend forever."

Netty Schwarz Vanderpol was also born in Amsterdam and spent fourteen months in Terezin, a concentration camp in Czechoslovakia. She had done needlepoint for many years, mainly on canvases designed by others. After hearing Elie Wiesel speak in 1984 she felt the

Figure 2-7
". . . and all the King's men . . . ,"
needlepoint and collage, 15″ × 22″, by
Netty Vanderpol. *Photography by Clive
Russ.*

importance of telling what she had experienced and so began to experiment with canvases of her own design based on Holocaust themes.

What started as an expression of personal feelings and memories took on the larger purpose of educating others and resulted in a suite of more than fifteen compelling pieces collectively entitled "Every Stitch a Memory." In a review of Netty's work in the *Christian Science Monitor* (March 1989), Marilyn Gardner wrote: "Here is no graphic portrayal of gas chambers of Auschwitz. . . . Instead, through the texture of yarn, . . . the interplay of colors, and the symbolic representation of places and events, these understated works give new and surprisingly powerful expressions to age-old themes of war, brutality and loss." Netty Vanderpol says that the work in Fig. 2-7 was made in memory of her mother, "who survived the camps, but was never truly whole again. The cracked mirror symbolizes the fragmented lives that Holocaust survivors experience. The diagonal blue bands, though becoming lighter as the years pass, never lose their melancholy."

In her quilt "From the Ghetto to Yerushalaim," Pamela Rishfeld uses a yellow star to begin her story. By gradually changing its color and that of the background she has poetically encapsulated an intense period of the history of the Jewish people. The quilt was made as a gift for her husband, a survivor of the Holocaust (see Color Plate 9).

The yellow star, barbed wire, butterflies, and flames, symbols of the Holocaust, have been used by many artists. Deborah Kelman's felt construction, *"Ein Sof"* (There is no end), reminds us that ethnic cleansing is not unique to this century (see Color Plate 8). After the defeat of Bar Kokhba in 135 C.E., the Romans forbade the teaching of the Torah. Many sages were put to death, among them Hanina ben

Teradyon, the head of the academy at Sikni in Galilee. He was wrapped in wet fleece and a Torah scroll and then set on fire. The fleece was to prolong his suffering by keeping his heart cool. When his students saw his agony they cried, "Rabbi, tell us, what do you see" "*Ein sof,*" he replied. "There is no end. I am dying but the letters fly to Heaven!"

My fascination with Spain started during the last years of the Second World War in my mother's Bronx kitchen. She was always listening to the war news on the radio, hoping that somehow there would be a clue to the whereabouts of the parents and siblings left behind in Poland. We heard an account of Jews in a small town who went to the synagogue for safety; the Nazis burned it down and shot anyone who tried to escape. My mother concluded that the same thing must have happened to our family. Eventually we learned from a cousin, who had in fact escaped just such a scene and watched the conflagration from a hiding place in the woods, that my mother's imaginings were very close to the truth. I asked her if there had ever been a time and place when Jews were accepted and safe. And my mother told me about the Golden Age of Spain, when the Jews lived in peace and prosperity alongside the Christians and the Moslems. "Just like in America," she said reassuringly.

I knew when I started this book that I wanted to include some-

Figure 2-8
Spanish patchwork *matzo* cover.

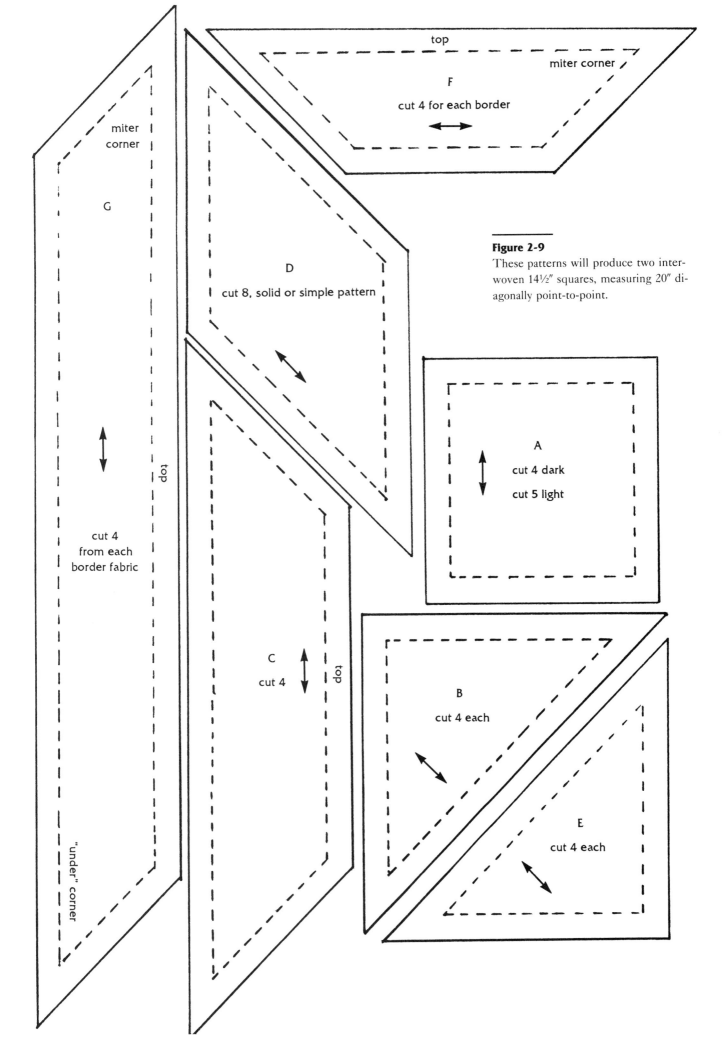

top

miter corner

F

cut 4 for each border

miter corner

G

D

cut 8, solid or simple pattern

Figure 2-9
These patterns will produce two interwoven 14½″ squares, measuring 20″ diagonally point-to-point.

A

cut 4 dark

cut 5 light

top

cut 4
from each
border fabric

C

cut 4

top

B

cut 4 each

"under" corner

E

cut 4 each

Figure 2-10
Assembly and quilting.

thing based on Spanish motifs. Even though my family background is not Sefardic, my affinity for Spanish-Jewish history and culture was given the opportunity to develop during the years I lived in Argentina and Spain. It was not, however, until seeing the *Convivencia* (Living Together) exhibition at the Jewish Museum in New York that the perfect motif presented itself. There I saw the early fourteenth-century Mocatta haggadah where the *matzo* was drawn as an elaborate interlocked eight-pointed star. *Matzot* in the form of overlapping squares and interlaced outlines with many variations appeared on several other of the haggadot shown, as well as on a fifteenth-century octagonal wooden box inlaid with ivory and gilt bronze. The show catalog described the decorative motif of the eight-pointed star "as commonly found on works of art from Spain, on textiles, ceramics and . . . on the pages of Hebrew manuscripts where it was used to represent the *matzo* in Passover haggadot."

The design on the wooden box called to me across the centuries and spoke to my inclination toward Hispano-Moorish decoration and my madness for patchwork. *The matzo* in the fourteenth-century Catalonian, Poblet haggadah, is rendered as a six-pointed interlaced star and painted in light and dark shades of violet and green. Thus my color scheme.

As you can see from Fig. 2-9 (see also Color Plate 10), I used a border design fabric for the interlocking square. Floral elements from the same fabric were used as part of the central nine-patch block. A gentle green, grape-leaf pattern fabric was used for the rest of the center, the binding, and the backing, and to make a three-pocket envelope on the back to hold the three ceremonial *mazot*. The remaining background fabrics were those from my stash, which complemented the border fabric.

Assemble the center nine-patch first, then add the corner triangles. To add the border carefully proceed around the central square so that the lines are straight. The quilting lines were meant to suggest *matzo* and were done in contrasting thread for that purpose. Thin polyester batting used for cloth children's books was used for the filling layer.

After quilting, trim excess batting and lining fabric. Bind the raw edge using a 1¼″-wide strip of the lining fabric or of a contrasting material. Cut this binding strip across the grain (meaning from selvage to selvage) of your fabric. It is stretchy and flexible this way and less likely to ripple than bias strips. (When cut lengthwise the fabric is stronger and more stable, which is good for borders but not for binding). You will appreciate the stretchiness of the cross-cut binding strips as you negotiate both the pointed corners and the reverse inside corners.

The Eastern European Jewish immigrants who streamed into America at the turn of the century thought they were arriving in the land of opportunity, the country whose streets were paved with gold. Although it wasn't so easy, American Jews have done well here, yet they have only been in the United States in significant numbers for about

Figure 2-11
"Scraps," as they are known to collectors of paper ephemera, were the forerunners of contemporary greeting cards. This one was printed by Hebrew Publishing in 1909.

Figure 2-12
"Pillow from Galicia," mixed media by Lonnie Stern Boninger. The transfer process used by Lonnie has reversed the scrap's image. *Photograph by Robert Sands.*

100 years. Yes, there were Jews in Colonial America; a case can even be made for Jewish input into Columbus's voyage. But in terms of significant numbers, and of meaning for the Jewish people as a whole, Jewish impact on America and America's impact in turn is a recent phenomenon.

The figure of Columbia in the 1909 scrap in Fig. 2-11 wearing a cap with the name "America" written in Yiddish on it. She is holding a key in one hand and with the other is opening the gates for immigrants obviously from Eastern Europe. The tiny inscription at the bottom is from Psalms and says, "Open up to me the gates of righteousness; I shall enter and give praise." It is with this expectation of fairness and the readiness to give praise and patriotism in return that the families of America's Jews arrived on these shores.

Lonnie Stern Boninger has cleverly used the image from this scrap as the centerpiece for her "Pillow from Galacia." Her "Family Hallah Cover" in Fig. 2-13, which also employs the photo transfer technique, includes pictures of four generations. The appliquéd lace is from her grandmother's wedding dress, which was given to her at the age of twelve. The inscription is in both Hebrew and English: "And the children of Israel shall keep the Sabbath, to observe the Sabbath throughout their generations, for an everlasting covenant."

Figure 2-13
"Family *Hallah* Cover," mixed media by Lonnie Stern Boninger. *Photograph by Robert Sands.*

Using a classical American sampler format and a new computer program, Emma Root also pays textile homage to multiple generations of her family. She says that sewing on her "Genealogy Sampler" was a prayer of thanks to her mother and grandmothers, who taught her how to hold a needle and to sew. The poem "Love is the thread that binds our lives in a lasting fabric, which time shall fray . . . only to be rewoven by each generation" is by Rabbi Chaim Stern in *The Gates of Prayer*. Emma's pattern is included here for your personal interpretation (not for commercial exploitation).

Like Lonnie Stern Boninger's grandmother, my parents immigrated to America.

Figure 2-14
"Genealogy Sampler," counted cross-stitch by Emma Root.

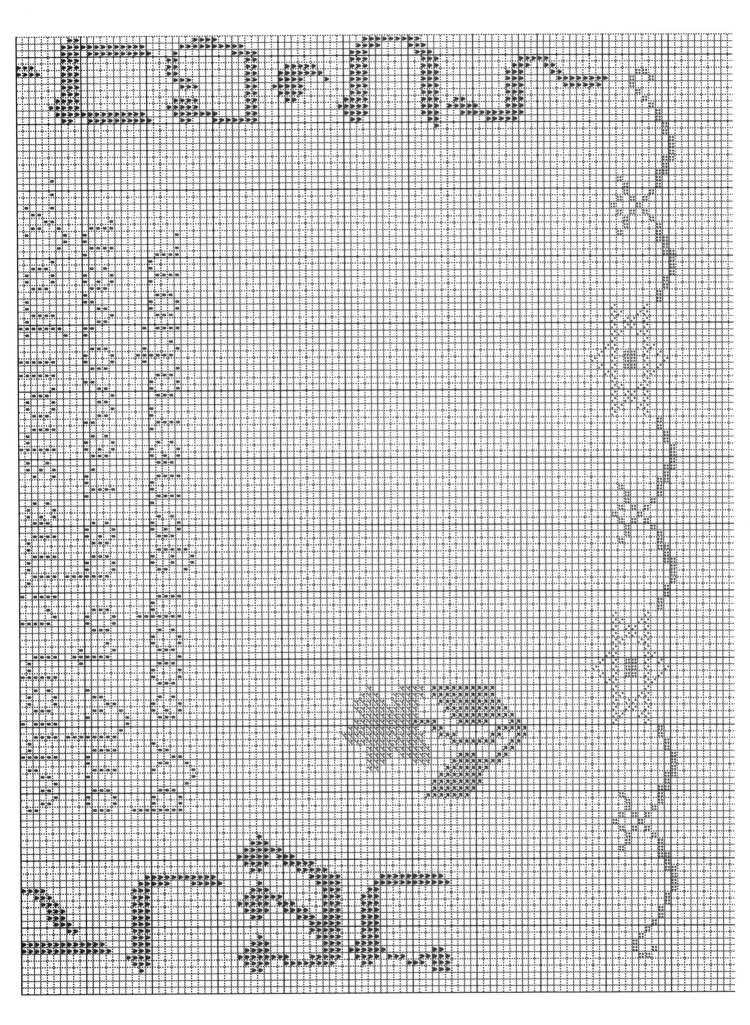

Figure 2-15 (overleaf)
Computer-generated pattern for "Genealogy Sampler," by Emma Root. Fill in
your own family names in the space below the poem. Pattern here is at 50% of
original; enlarge 200% to get the size
Emma used.

#	Sym	Description	#Used	(sq. in.)
1.	⁄	light pink	803	4.751
2.	⊏	brown	223	1.320
3.	₮	blue	1610	9.527
4.	::	golden brown	160	0.947
5.	⌒	gold	267	1.580
6.	8	dark pink	1018	6.024
7.	⌄	green	940	5.562
8.	·.	straw yellow	304	1.799

My mother came at the age of sixteen with her brother, leaving her
parents behind.

My father (seated on right with book in Fig. 2-16) had his bar
mitzvah on the boat. Grandfather David (my father's father) had
arrived years before and, after deciding that New York City was not

Figure 2-16
Bobeh Raisel and her five sons.

Figure 2-17
Bobeh Raisel's bedspread, 84″ × 84″ plus fringe.

Figure 2-18
Detail of *Bobeh* Raisel's bedspread.

the place for a *shtetle bucher* (village boy) to live, hitchhiked to Rockland, Maine. With thirty dollars investment capital, he started as an "I-cash-clothes man," pushing a wheelbarrow through the streets and giving people pennies for their old clothes and rags, which he then sold to paper mills. Eventually he branched out to scrap metal and finally saved enough money for steamship tickets for his family. By then, his wife, my *Bobeh* Raisel, and their two oldest sons had died of typhoid. All I have of my grandmother is this picture and the bedspread she crocheted and embroidered. Her mother, my great-grandmother, brought the bedspread to America along with the remaining sons, which included my father. It was crocheted in a filet stitch with black cotton thread. Bright multicolored woolen yarn was then woven into the crocheted grid in a pattern of encircled flowers and Russian/Ukrainian words in the Cyrillic alphabet. The phrase says, "Made by a Woman's Hand, Year 1909," and to that is added, in Cyrillic letters, R.S. (Raisel Schechter).

Studying the spread to see how it was made, learning how to weave multicolored yarn through the grid, and figuring out how *Bobeh* Raisel made her fringes was an intense experience that brought me close to the grandmother I never knew as I tried to imagine her life

Figure 2-19
"*Meshuge Hallah* Cover." Crazy quilt
Sabbath bread cover made in honor of
all the wonderful and *meshugener* family
events of 1992.

through the work of her hands. Because a number of us worked on the lap robe, it bears the initials of Helen Tupa, Ann Kaplan, Linda Urbach, and myself, as well as the phrase "The Work of Our Hands, 1993" (see Color Plate 12).

Somewhere in the third grade I learned about the Pilgrims, their coming to the New World, and their samplers and patchwork quilts. Since sewing was already important in my life, it became imperative to me that I make a sampler, hoping to become more American in the process. I think I did.

Twenty-five years ago, while living in Madrid with two young sons, I decided to make each of them an album quilt that would incorporate our family's American, Jewish, and Spanish experiences. I've always been intrigued by crazy quilts and have collected several old ones, but I've never made one of my own. This seemed the perfect year to try my hand. With my writing a book, and with my two youngest children getting married within two weeks of one another, the year qualified as a bit *meshuge*—fun and gratifying, but definitely "crazy."

I decided to make a new family *hallah* cover with the peace of

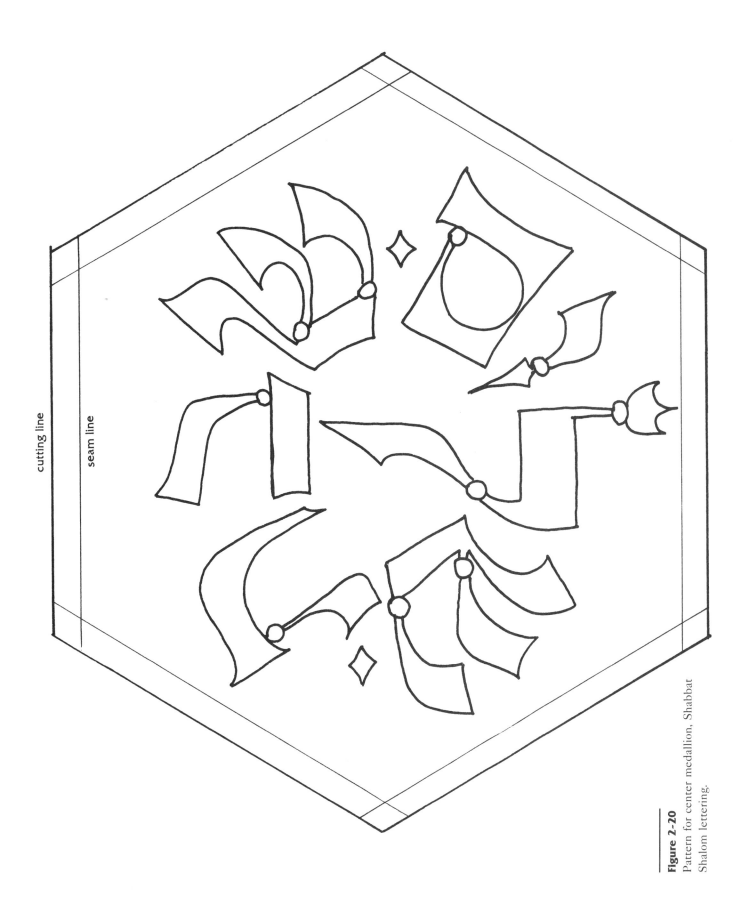

cutting line

seam line

Figure 2-20
Pattern for center medallion, Shabbat
Shalom lettering.

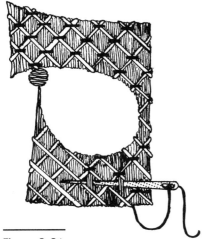

Figure 2-21
Laid and trellis-couched embroidery.

Shabbat symbolized by a white *magen David* in the center and bright and dark colors in the surrounding pieces to represent the work week. It was fun looking for fabrics. My husband sacrificed a tie patterned with the two biblical spies carrying a huge cluster of grapes to the project. Blue denim from some old jeans was also used. The star was assembled first, using seven different pale, or white-on-white, fabrics. Shabbat Shalom was embroidered on the center hexagon using a laid-and-couched stitch. Ivory-colored pearl cotton was used, with a metallic multicolored thread for the couching. When the center star was embroidered and assembled, I played with the other accumulated fabric pieces until they were the right sizes, shapes, proportions, and positions and then stitched them to a muslin backing larger than the finished piece would be. After the star was pinned in place the fun part began of embroidering the seams and intersections with all of the stitches I could think of or was in the mood for at the time. It was a great piece of pickup work to do while preparing for the weddings, and it now reminds us of the special year when we all became family (see Color Plate 11).

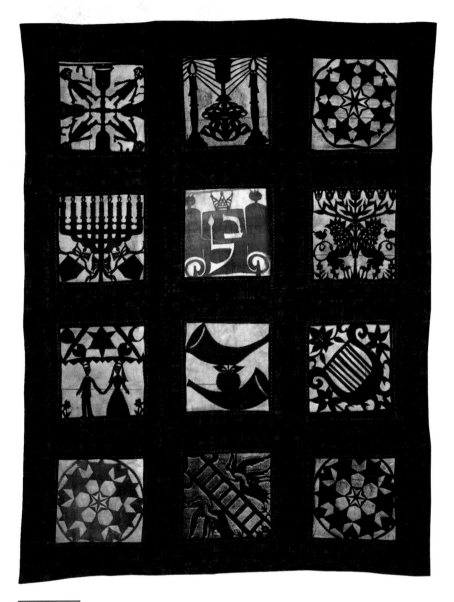

Plate 1
"Paper-cut Blueprint Quilt" by Lynne
Lederman, 38″ × 50″.

Plate 2
"Strong as a Lion" ark curtain for The
Elmont Jewish Center children's cha-
pel, Elmont, New York.

Plate 3 (opposite)
"And Grant Thee Peace" by the author, 96″ × 106″. Silkscreened fabric, machine pieced and hand quilted.

Plate 4
"Adam and Eve" by the author, 42″ × 54″. Hand appliqued wall hanging.

Plate 5
"Moses" by Miriam K. Sokoloff, 50″ × 37″. Hand appliqued and quilted wall hanging. *Photograph by Hillel Burger.*

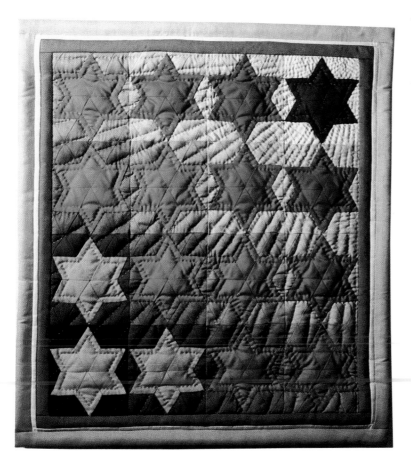

Plate 9
"From the Ghetto to Yerushalaim" by
Pamela Rishfeld, 21″ × 23″. *Photograph
courtesy of the artist.*

Plate 10
"Sefardic" *matzo* cover by the author
(see directions in Part Two).

Plate 11
Crazy *hallah* cover by the author (see directions in Part Two).

Plate 12

Bobeh Raisel's bedspread returns as a laprobe. Crochet grid by Helen Tupa, flowers by Ann Kaplan, fringes by Linda Urbach and author. Shown with author's daughter Keren as a doll.

PART THREE

The Present

Once there was a poor seamstress who had been orphaned
as a child, and widowed as a young mother, and knew only
a life of drudgery. Nevertheless, as she stitched from dawn
into the night she sang. Sometimes aloud and sometimes in
a whisper. Year after year she sewed and sang. The
garments which came from her hands were many and
varied. She repaired a farmer's overalls as carefully as she
embroidered a bridal gown. Yet the song that she sang
remained the same; it really wasn't a song at all. Over and
over to whatever melody came to mind she sang the letters
of the Alphabet. Finally her neighbors, amazed at the
endless variety with which she sang the same letters, asked
her why she sang no other song, and she replied: "I have
always wanted to be learned. To sit in the study house and
the house of prayer, to understand the order of the universe
and to pray to the Master of us all. Yet it has been my lot
to learn only the Alphabet. And so each day I give back to
the Lord what has been given to me and with His greater
understanding and compassion He can form the letters into
prayers and praises to suit Himself."

Adapted from a Hasidic Story

Figure 3-1
"The Alphabet Song," silkscreen print.

The Alphabet Song

There is an old Chinese curse that says, "May you live in interesting times!" We certainly do; but sometimes it is for us to decided whether we are cursed or blessed. Like the seamstress in the story, we must use our best skills to improve the world, and then take the next day as it comes, leaving the balance in Other Hands.

The projects in this section reflect our involvement in family and community life as well as contemporary issues. Creating potential heirlooms can provide both tactile and spiritual solace as we deal with today's challenges.

> *Judaism begins in the home. . . . It begins in homes where Jewish words re-echo, where the Jewish book is honored, where the Jewish song is heard. Judaism begins in homes where the child sees and participates in symbols and rites which link him to a people and a culture. It begins in homes where the Jewish etching or painting and Jewish ceremonial objects are visible and exercise a silent influence upon those who behold them.*
>
> *Rabbi Morris Adler*

There was no question that my parents' Bronx apartment was Jewish. It *sounded, smelled, and tasted* Jewish because we spoke, cooked, and ate Eastern European Yiddish. And it looked Jewish with the *mezuzah* on the doorpost and the tin Hanukkah lamp on top of the refrigerator. The apartment felt even more Jewish on Thursday nights when my mother washed the floors. Because there were four of us in four small rooms, she covered the wet floors with newspapers to protect them while they were drying. Those newspapers were the first sign of Shabbos as my sister and I traipsed off to bed each Thursday night.

Today, my interior design clients ask, "How can my home look Jewish in an American Country or Italian Contemporary style?" Architect Mies van der Rohe, the celebrated proponent of minimalism, said, "God is in the details." I couldn't agree more. In this design era of "post-modernism," eclecticism and ethnicity are "in." The free use of a variety of styles that harmoniously coexist is as easy to live with as it is fashionable. Today's Judaica artists and craftspeople are creating a stream of inspiring decorative and ceremonial objects to fill our homes and to inspire our own work.

Two hallmarks of the Jewish home are the *mezuzah* and the *mizrah*. The *mezuzah*, which in Hebrew means "doorpost," is a small parchment scroll, hand lettered with Deuteronomy 6:4–9 and 11:13–21, placed in a case, and affixed to the doorpost as a sign of identity and a reminder of belief. In ancient days, the container was a reed but it can be of any material. They are usually made of metal, clay, or wood, but

Figure 3-2
Mezuzah, batik velveteen with beads, quilted, 3½″ × 12″, by Deborah Kelman. *Photograph courtesy of the artist.*

mezuzot can also provide a challenging project for textile work. The blue and white quilted, batik velvet *mezuzah* case by California artist Deborah Kelman in Fig. 3-2 incorporates wood, silver, brass, copper, coconut shell, buffalo horn, and ceramic beads to signify the bond between the earth and its Creator. The name *Shaddai*, in Hebrew an acronym of the phrase "Guardian of the doorposts of Israel," is commonly found on *mezuzot*. There is a diagonally stitched pocket on the back of the top section to hold the parchment scroll. Because of the materials used, Deborah's *mezuzah* cannot be put on an outside door unless it is protected from the weather. It is ideally suited for a large contemporary archway.

Projects: Home, Holidays, Community

I made the paper-cut "Bobeh and Me" when my daughter was a little girl and my mother was still alive. Designed as a *mizrah* using domestic motifs, it celebrates the special relationship of my daughter and mother. Although it is a special marker for the eastern wall, the *mizrah* is a uniquely Jewish ornament suitable for any room in your house. The word *mizrah* originally meant "rising of the sun"; now it means "east." When the Temple stood, people praying there faced the Holy of Holies. In other parts of Jerusalem they turned in the direction of the Temple. Outside of Jerusalem they faced the Holy City. The custom grew up in the diaspora of marking the eastern wall as a sign of mourning for the destroyed Temple. Sometimes this was accomplished by omitting some plaster or a stone. More often, though, decorative techniques and ornaments were used. *Mizrahim* have been, and can be, made as paintings and plaques in any technique and material from paper and plastic to precious metals and, of course, textiles. Most of the motifs in this book are suitable for a *mizrah*. If you want to make a simple one, with only the word, use any of the alef-bets shown in Part One. A traditional symbol to include is the seven-branched *menorah* framed with a pair of columns.

For years, I had wanted to interpret the "Bobeh and Me" paper-cut in appliqué and embroidery; writing this book gave me an excuse to do so. As I worked on the *mizrah* I debated with myself which chapter to include it in: Past or Future. Then, when my grand-daughter, five-year-old Jessica, saw it, her first question was, "Could that be you and me?" Her next question was, "Can I have it?" Battling with vanity, I agreed to both. (The spelling of *bobeh* has become anglicized: "Bubbie Mae"—her other grandmother is "Bubbie Millie"). Jessica wanted the appliqué for her room, she assured me, and when she gets married she is taking it with her. The *mizrah* above the table in the piece was made from a scrap of cross-stitched tablecloth made by my mother's mother. I embroidered the Hebrew letters over

Figure 3-4
"*Bobeh* and Me" *mizrah*, detail: Sabbath
candlesticks and *hamentashen*.

Figure 3-3
"*Bobeh* and Me," paper-cut.

the flowers and "framed" it by couching metallic gold cord in place
(see Color Plate 13).

At the same Pomegranate Guild meeting where Lynne Lederman
saw the paper-cuts that began her blueprint quilt (see Color Plate 1),
Sarah Neckes decided to interpret the "Bobeh and Me" paper-cut
mizrah in crewel embroidery.

The five-part needlepoint *mizrah* shown in Fig. 3-6 was designed
by Alice Nussbaum for the Halpern family of Rochester, New York, in
collaboration with Noreen Halpern whose Judaica knowledge and
family insights were invaluable to the design process. Phrases from the

Figure 3-5
Sarah Neckes starting her embroidered
version of the paper-cut.

Bible and from *Pirke Avot* (Sayings of the Father) were chosen based
on each family member's interests and traits. Symbols based on these
quotations and on personal favorite themes were added. The phrase
bordering the center panel says, "There are three crowns: the crown of
the Torah, the crown of the priesthood and the crown of royalty, but
the crown of a good name surpasses them all" (*Pirke Avot*, 4:7). In the
center, the Hebrew letters that spell Halpern have been formed as a
crown with the negative spaces spelling *mizrah*.

The *mizrah* is worked on 13-mesh canvas using the continental
stitch for most of the piece. DMC perle cotton thread was chosen,
rather than wool, because of its sheen and vibrant colors. The piece is
32″ square and each of the five panels are to be hung on the wall,
exactly 1″ apart. This design required meticulous counting of stitches.
When Alice paints a canvas, it is stitch-exact so that the embroiderer
knows just where to put her needle. She made the following needlepoint recommendations:

Figure 3-6
Halpern family *mizrah*, 32″ × 32″, designed by Alice Nussbaum. Needlepoint embroidery by Noreen Halpern. *Photograph by David R. Halpern.*

"Use the best quality canvas available, usually 13-mesh mono, non-interlock. Non-interlock canvas makes it easier to paint stitch-exact. Use 18-mesh for smaller, softer items such as *kipot*. These sizes accommodate the largest variety of fibers: silk, wool, cotton, metallics. Use only permanent sketching pens specifically made for fabrics or canvas. To paint a canvas use permanent acrylics."

It has often been said that "more than the Jews have kept the Sabbath, the Sabbath has kept the Jews." From the very beginning, the Sabbath was observed with joy and celebration as well as with rest. During the Babylonian exile, and since the destruction of the Second Temple in 70 C.E., the Sabbath—which, because it is so essentially personal and domestic, was easier to carry into exile than the three pilgrimage festivals of Sukkot, Passover, and Shavuot—grew in intensity and became the mainstay of Jewish life. The home table became the alter, and every Jew a priest. When Jews lived in ghettos, Sabbath observance was a magic island of spiritual retreat in a sea of hostility. In today's world, where the only thing that is certain is the very speed of change, we too can greatly benefit from such a refuge.

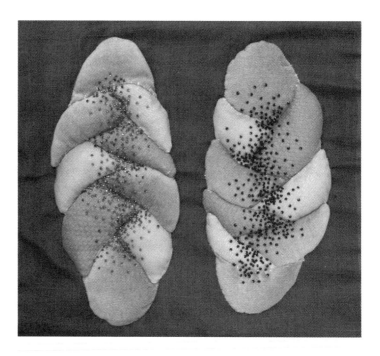

Figure 3-7
Hallah cover, stuffed, appliquéd, and beaded, by Rivkah Weil.

The braided and glazed bread eaten at the Sabbath meal is called *hallah*. Two breads are customarily used because it is said that when the Jews were wandering in the desert after escaping from slavery in Egypt, a double ration of manna fell before the Sabbath so that God could also rest. A *hallah* cover is put over the breads while the candles are lit and the blessing over the wine is said. Legend says that the

Figure 3-8
Daisy *hallah* cover.

hallah cover represents the dew that covered the manna in the desert. Another legend says that the *hallah* cover keeps God from becoming "confused" because the opening prayers are said before blessing the bread.

I would rather make *hallah* covers than any other needlework project (except maybe quilts). At present I am working on three *hallah* covers, one for each of my children. As I mentioned earlier, for my daughter I am embroidering Sabbath angels. My oldest son is a dedicated fisherman, so his *hallah* cover has on it the Leviathan, the primordial monster fish of the deep, upon which the righteous will feast when the Messiah comes. For newly married Jeffrey and Liana, I am working on a multicolored version of the *hallah* cover shown in Fig. 3-8, which, using the flower alef-bet in Part One (see Fig. 1-17), simply says: "*Hallah*." For Jeffrey and Liana's *hallah* cover, the daisies are various shades of blue, purple, and pink, and the inscription says: "Shabbat Shalom, Sabbath Peace." Use the elements you like from the drawing in Fig. 3-9 and words of your choice for your *hallah* cover.

Recycling, a politically correct buzzword these days, comes naturally to needleworkers and quilters who are by their nature addicted to salvaging every scrap and thread to use in some future project. When my mother came to this country as a girl of sixteen, she brought with her a trunk full of hand-embroidered linens and petticoats. Because petticoats were considered unfashionable here, she sent them back to Poland where they were destroyed together with our family. Perhaps that is why I haunt flea markets and yard sales, looking for doilies and other bits of handwork that can be turned into *hallah* and *matzo* covers. Finding these pieces is a little like finding lost relatives. The daisy *hallah* cover in Fig. 3-8 was once such a doily, bought for six dollars in Bucksport, Maine. The doily served to inspire me to create the flower alef-bet so that I could embroider the Hebrew in letters that matched the flowers.

Passover is the oldest continually celebrated religious ceremony in the world. It is so old that its exact origins, and even the meaning of the word *pesah*, are shrouded in history. The symbols and customs of all holidays are always much older than their interpretations. As we sit at the seder table, retelling our ancient origin stories and explaining the symbolic foods, all the epochs of Jewish history are there simultaneously. We suspend time, and through ritual, songs, food, a bit of theater, and sense memory, experience the liberation from Egyptian bondage, which becomes symbolic of all slaveries, past and present.

My husband Myron Tupa's great-grandparents came to this country from Bohemia and Moravia and settled into farming communities around Silver Lake, Minnesota. Part of the family still farms and other family members live in town. Myron grew up in Glencoe, Minnesota, in a little house much like my parents' Bronx apartment. There, my

Figure 3-9
Daisy pattern.

Figure 3-10
Matzo cover.

mother-in-law, Helen Tupa, a woman ahead of her times, raised her two children in a house with no indoor plumbing, and made the family's clothes, baked bread, tended the garden, canned the produce for the long Minnesota winters, and held down a full-time job. She taught in a one-room schoolhouse. Myron remembers her, even in the fifties, driving their Model A Ford to work in the earliest hours of the winter mornings in order to start the fire in the coal stove before the children arrived.

Figure 3-11
Passover pillows recycled from Helen Tupa's embroidered flour-sack dish towels.

The flour for the bread, poppy-seed-filled *bukhtah* and *kolachi* (Czechoslovakian pastries), came in huge patterned and plain muslin sacks, fabric too good to waste. It was made—recycled—into dishtowels and children's clothes. In her spare time Helen crocheted and embroidered. She ordered iron-on embroidery designs from the newspaper and, using the flour sacks, made "fancy" dish towels. On our last visit to Glencoe we found them neatly ironed and saved in the attic and decided to bring them back into the family circle where they belonged. The dish towels with their simple cross-stitched kitchen motifs of soup, salt shakers, wine glasses, pitcher, and kittens had been

Figure 3-12
Cooking kitten pattern.

Figure 3-13
Wine glasses pattern.

waiting there in the attic to be dressed up for Passover (see Color Plate 14).

The dish towels, wine glasses, soup, salt shakers, and cooking kitten needed no modification to be made into pillowcases (Fig. 3-11). The cross-stitched pitcher was cut out and appliquéd in place with a buttonhole stitch onto a larger towel, my grandchildren's hands were outline stitched, and a running stitch was used to form water. The former dish towel was turned into a Passover hand towel (see Fig. 3-17). The two singing kittens were easily turned into the "Four Question Kids" (see Fig. 3-18). For the *Afikomen* bag I turned the cooking kitten into the "simple" child, and created a naughty kitten to represent the disaffected fourth son to whom the Passover story is explained (see Fig. 3-19). Because none of the dish towels had a motif that could be used for the *matzo* cover, I drew the design in Fig. 3-20, incorporating the flowers and stitches from the other towels.

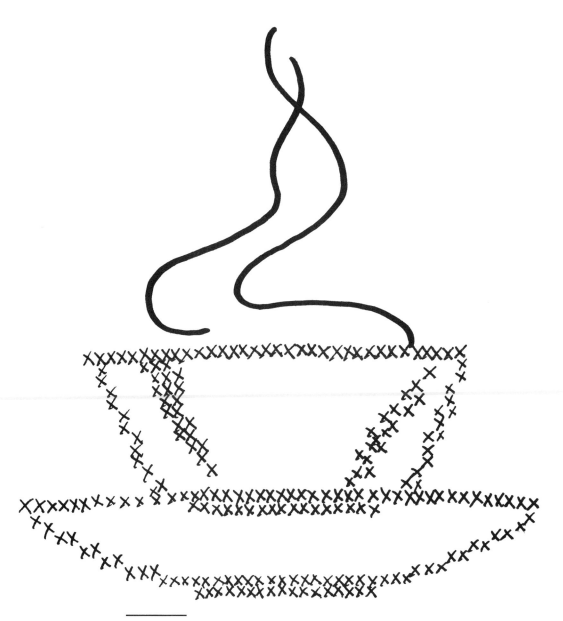

Figure 3-14
Soup bowl pattern.

The borders, made from prewashed, 100% cotton prints in shade of green, white, and tan, were cut 1½″ wide, allowing for ¼″ seam allowances, with a rotary cutter and then strip pieced. The pillowcases have European envelope backs for easy removal. Two pieces of light weight green cotton fabric, together with the backing, form three pockets for the ceremonial *matzot* held by the *matzo* cover.

Passover exists concurrently in all times and all places. For an elegant contemporary approach to *matzo* cover design, consider the work of the well-known New York textile artist Ina Golub in Fig. 3-21. Ina has skillfully appliquéd gold metallic fabric to a textured white

Figure 3-15
Salt and pepper shaker pattern.

cotton base. Her choices of fabric and the beautifully formed letters add another dimension to experiencing pesah.

The Sabbath sustains us and Passover defines us, but, in the words of the rabbis of the Talmud (*Tractate Shabbat* 21b), "What is Hanukkah?" More than 1,800 years ago the sages compiling the Talmud questioned the custom of lighting lamps in celebration of Hanukkah. Today we need to rethink the issues involved as Hanukkah changes from a low-key holiday to a major ethnic celebration and make certain it is understood in authentic Jewish terms, rather than as the Jewish version of a substitute for Christmas. Hanukkah, which commemorates both a military and a spiritual victory, celebrates the first recorded battle for religious freedom. When the Maccabees rededicated the Temple, the victory was not merely against foreign domination; it was also a triumph of the human spirit over the luring and compelling forces of materialism and conformity. Since the first Hanukkah celebration twenty-one centuries ago, every generation has been inspired by the message of Hanukkah to resist temptations and tyrants that have arisen. That the people and nation of Israel survive to this day is testimony to the enduring quality of that ancient miracle.

In my Bronx childhood Hanukkah was a quiet, homey holiday. Orange candles were lit in the tin Hanukkah lamp on top of the

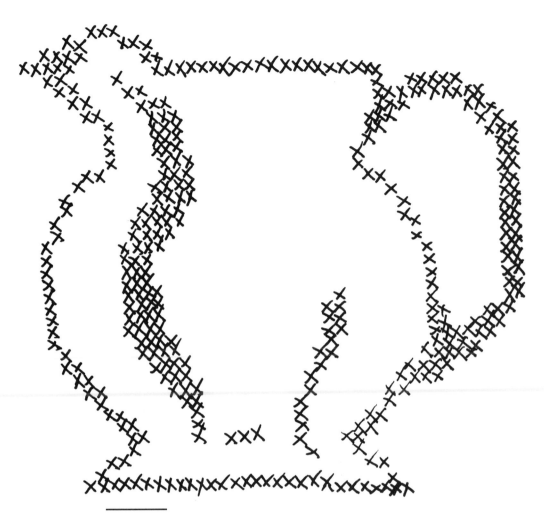

Figure 3-16
Pitcher pattern.

refrigerator. At the Yiddish school I attended every afternoon after public school, we presented a Hanukkah program of songs, dances, and poetry for our parents. One year, nine of us dressed up in sheets and paper crowns and, holding candles as torches, became Statues of Liberty. We stood in a row, and as the child-statue designated as the *shamash* lit our candles, we each recited a line from Emma Lazarus' poem "The New Colossus":

> Give me your tired, your poor,
> Your huddled masses yearning to breathe free
> The wretched refuse of your teeming shore.

That poem was about us. Our parents had immigrated to the Land of the Free. We were the wretched refuse and we were breathing free. It was a wonderful feeling!

Years later, when my sons were teenagers and my daughter still in elementary school, I made the "Ms. Liberty Enlightens the World"

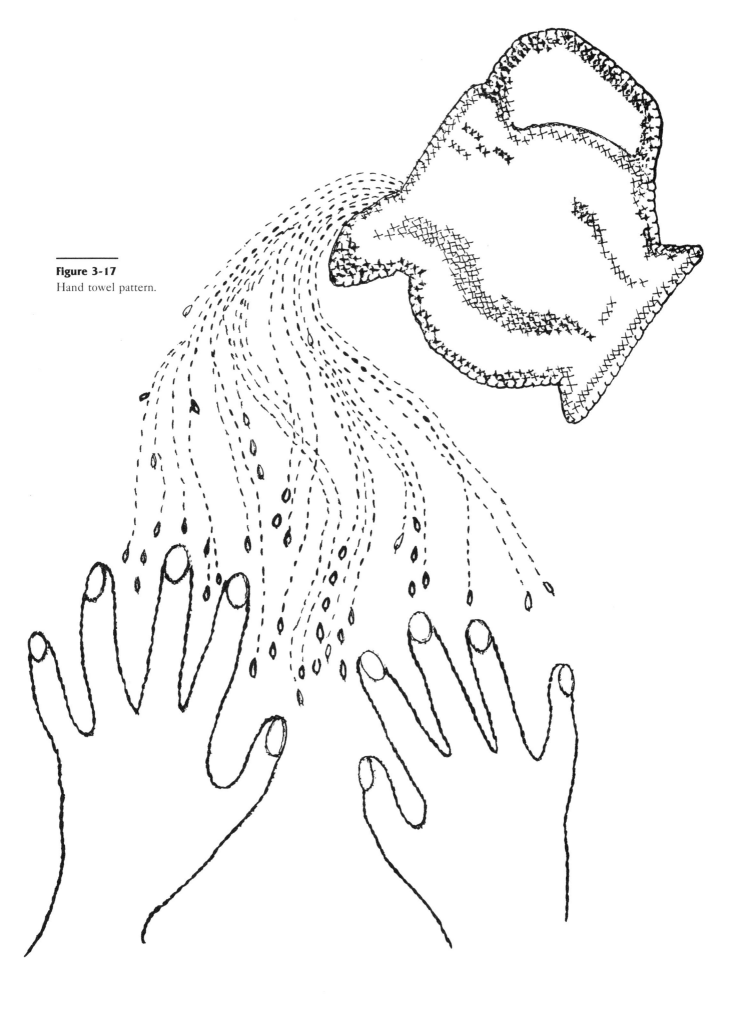

Figure 3-17
Hand towel pattern.

Figure 3-18
"Four Questions Kids" pattern.

Figure 3-19
Afikomen bag pattern.

Figure 3-20
Matzo cover pattern.

Figure 3-21
Matzo cover, cotton and metallic applique, by Ina Golub. Courtesy of Hilda Kaspin. *Photograph by Erik Landsberg.*

Figure 3-22
"Ms. Liberty Enlightens The World" Hankukkah lamp, 1974. *Photograph by Bill Arou.*

Figure 3-23
Statue of Liberty Hanukkah lamps.

Figure 3-24

Consider doing a smaller project using only the *shamas* and the first candle and
changing some of the stars to yellow Stars of David on a black or dark gray field,
or use a different verse from the poem, and so on.

Hanukkah lamp, shown in Fig. 3-22, for our annual Hanukkah *latke* party. It was made from plastic souvenirs of the Statue of Liberty and birthday candle holders arranged on wooden two-by-fours covered with flags. Imagine my surprise and delight when the Jewish Museum in New York included it in their exhibt of Jewish-American folk art and then kept it for their permanent collection.

Because the museum acquired the lamp and a collector bought the replacement I made a few years later, I decided to do a two-dimensional version of my childhood theatrical debut. As you can see in Color Plate 15 the work is still in progress. It is a big piece for needlepoint: 36″ × 17″. Caroline Levine is working on the project. She is using the painted canvas as a crib sheet for the location of the colors and embroidering the line-drawn canvas (noninterlocked). We decided it would be safer to use unpainted canvas in order to make certain that the white stripes remained white (even with the most permanent of markers there can be some rub off). Caroline is using primarily basket weave stitches for the figures and letters; a combination of tied cross-stitch, with cashmere and mosaic stitches for the statue bases, to suggest stone; and slanting gobelin for the stripes.

The drawings are here for your personal use. You can take the color photograph to a processor who has a flat bed scanner and can graph it for you in color, use an enlarging photocopier to get it to the size *you* are happy with, or measure it out and draw it block by block. Another idea is to enlarge a few of the statues, draw some of your own, and arrange them to suit yourself. Consider crewel embroidery or appliqué as well as needlepoint. You will notice that I have drawn each of the statues differently. This reflects the fact that Ms. Liberty hasn't and doesn't always face forward with her lamp lit. She has, in fact, turned her back at cruical times on aspiring immigrants.

Figure 3-25

Latke potholders by members of the Greater Boston Chapter of the Pomegranate Guild of Judaic Needlework.

Figure 3-26
"*Bobeh* and Me," crewel embroidery by Sarah Neckes, based on the paper-cut design in Fig. 3-3. Hanukkah candle and *dreidel* boxes embroidered on plastic canvas by Edith Shane.

Figure 3-27
Bureau scarf.

Our chapter of the Pomegranate Guild of Judaic Needlework dedicated the December meeting to a discussion of the topic "How to Decorate for Hanukkah Like a Jewish Mother." While we all agreed that is is not traditional to decorate for Hanukkah, we also recognized that Hanukkah is a holiday in transition and that, because we usually socialize more at the time of year, we might want to make things pretty. The challenge, of course, is to keep it authentic and to make it attractive or useful. We closed the meeting with a workshop in making *latke*-shaped potholders from prequilted fabrics in potato-pancake colors (some raw, some ready, some burnt). And Edith Shane and Sarah Neckes showed what they had made as Hanukkah presents for family members (see Fig. 3-26).

Figure 3-28
Lion and eagle drawing for scarf.

Fleet as a Deer

Bold as a Leopard

Figure 3-29
Deer and leopard drawing for scarf.

The Pomegranate Guild is a marvelous national organization that welcomes people of all levels of sewing skill and Jewish knowledge. Our group has members ranging in age from nine to ninety. For more information, see the national membership address in the Directory of Textile Artists at the back of the book.

Pursuing thoughts triggered by our Pomegranate meeting, I decided to make something for Hanukkah that would be both useful and fit naturally into our home. Every year at Hanukkah I pull out my large lamp collection and place the lamps all over the house. We don't light them all but enjoy looking at them and sharing them with visitors. At our annual *latke* party, however, we do light many of them in order to have as many people as possible participate in the lighting ceremony. Inevitably the furniture gets covered with dripping wax. Not being

Figure 3-30
Menorah drawing for scarf.

much of a fan of aluminum-foil doilies I decided to recycle a flea-market linen bureau scarf into some kind of protection for the dining room sideboard where most of the lamps are lit.

The four animals symbolize the virtues of the dedicated Jew described in *Pirke Avot* V.23, where we are enjoined to "be as strong as a lion, as swift as the eagle, fleet as the deer and bold as the leopard to do the will of your Father (Parent) in heaven." These four animals have been motifs in Jewish art for centuries. I borrowed my renditions of them from my dining room Tabris oriental rug. The animal patterns and the *menorah* are given here in the size that I embroidered them.

Fleet as a Deer

Bold as a Leopard

Strong as a Lion

Swift as an Eagle

Figure 3-31
Complete drawing for scarf.

Configure them as you like or use the drawing in Fig. 3-31 as a guide. Add foliage, salt, and pepper as desired.

Family identity and celebrations are the bedrock of our community and enrich our lives and ensure continuity. My father said that the Jews are like a *lokshen kugel*—noodle pudding—so mixed up together that it's impossible to tell where one begins and another ends. What affects one Jew affects us all. This is as true today as ever. We come together to pray, to celebrate, to mourn, to do good works. And to make art and sew.

We usually think of the *tallit*, prayer shawl, as a male-only garment. In Reform, Conservative, and Reconstructionist synagogues many women are now also wearing *tallitot* as well as *yarmulkah*-type head coverings. The *tallit* is usually a simple, woven striped rectangle of cloth with a decorative collar area and ritual fringes at the corners. While researching this book I found quite a few textile artists embellishing *tallitot* with embroidery, appliqué, and painting. The collection of *tallitot* shown in Fig. 3-32 was made by a group of three artists who sign their work collectively as "Larosh." Using exquisitely colored handwoven silks and trims, Larry Cryderman, Reeva Shaffer, and Shoshana Enosh create a full range of Judaica items from *kippot* and prayer shawls to ark curtains and wedding canopies.

Figure 3-32
Tallitot by Larosh. *Photograph courtesy of the artists.*

Using her many skills as fiber artist, folklorist, teacher, and nurse, Shirley Waxman went to Israel in April 1992 under the auspices of the American Association for Ethiopian Jews (AAEJ) to help new Israeli immigrant women from Ethiopia take steps toward earning a living. These women are part of the 14,000 immigrants who were dramatically brought to Israel during Operation Solomon in May 1991. Shirley arrived with boxes of thread and yards of fabric in order to start a self-sufficient cottage industry. There, in mobile homes near Mash'abbe Sade Nitzan in the Negev Desert, she taught Ethiopian-Jewish women to utilize their traditional embroidery stitches to create marketable items. The program started with fifteen women; by the time

Figure 3-33
Crochet silk *kippot* trimmed with beads, braid, and bows, by Larosh. *Photograph courtesy of the artists.*

she left forty were involved. Two months later there were ninety participants. With her strong background in folklore and textiles, Shirley was able to guide the group while fully respecting their indigenous skills, patterns, and sense of color.

Shirley's English was translated to Hebrew; a second translator then explained in Amharic (the native language of Ethiopians) the significance of skull caps and Sabbath bread covers, which are not a part of the Ethiopian-Jewish tradition. The women were encouraged to use their own designs and color combinations to make these items for the American market. The resulting *kippot* and *hallah* covers are brilliant in every sense of the word. Each piece is unique, embroidered in bright colors highlighted in black—a typical characteristic of Ethiopian needlework. The women are paid by the piece, and eventually the project ownership will be completely in their hands.

Recently Shirley was asked by Farbrengen, one of the older *chavurot* in the Washington, D.C., area to design and coordinate a memorial wall hanging with the Tree of Life as the central motif. Fifteen people with varying degrees of skill worked on this project, which commemorates the lives of members, friends, and relatives who have died. The striking results can be seen at the George Washington

Figure 3-34
Ethiopian *kippot* and *hallah* cover. *Photograph by Herb Pennock.*

University Hillel House where Farbrengen holds regular services. While working on group and social efforts, Shirley still finds time to make personal textiles for family and clients (see Fig. 3-35).

All over the country groups like Farbrengen are making quilts for many reasons. The Heimish-Amish Quilters in Van Nuys, California, began to meet several years ago to sew together on Tuesday nights. They auctioned their first Amish-inspired quilt for $1,700 and donated most of the money to an antinuclear arms group. They have gone on to make a pictorial album quilt honoring American women in government and the arts and are now working on a quilt with the theme of immigration and Ellis Island because most of the quilters have a parent who came to this country via that gateway.

The most famous and the most poignant group quilt in America now is The NAMES Project AIDS Memorial Quilt, which has already become an international symbol of the fight against AIDS. The NAMES Project provides a creative, positive form of expression for those whose

Plate 20
"In the Beginning," 66″ × 83″. One of a pair of appliqued quilts.

Plate 21

"Ani L'Dodi" (I Am My Beloved's) by Phyllis Kantor. Handwoven, embroidered, quilted and beaded. Made for Temple Sinai, Champaign, Illinois. *Photograph by Kent Peterson.*

Plate 22
"Kaleidoscopic IV: The Crystal Canopy" designed and pieced by Paula
Nadelstern, and hand quilted by Lynn Della Posta; 75″ × 85″. *Photograph by Bobby
Hansson.*

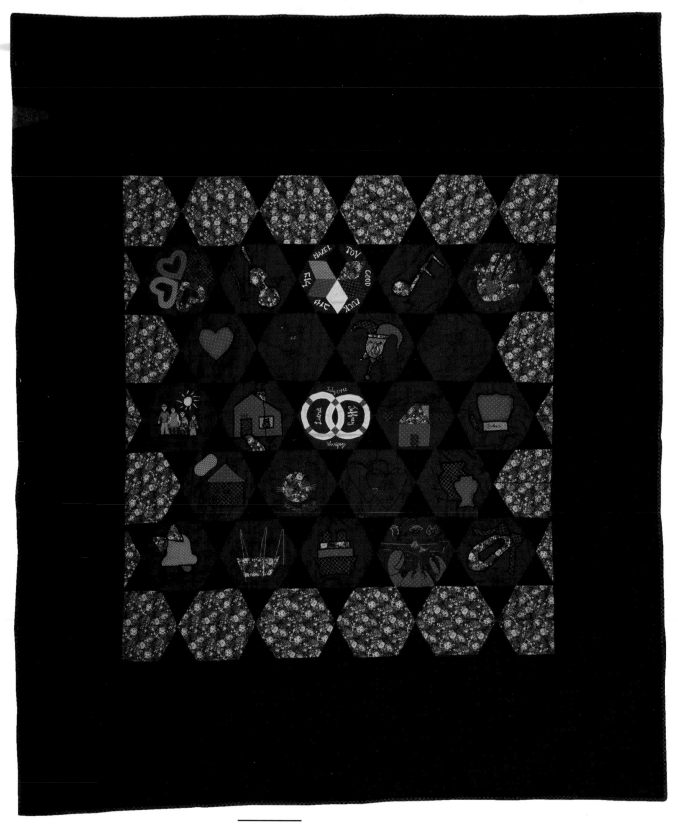

Plate 23
"Mazel Tov Huppah" family album quilt, 90″ × 104″. Hand and machine-embroidered and appliqued by the family of Jeffrey and Liana Rockland; handquilted by Mary Ann Flaud.

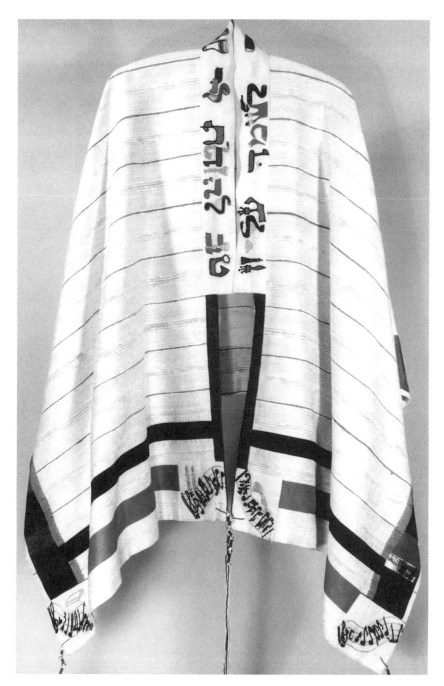

Figure 3-35
"*Tallit* for a Cantor," pieced bands of
fabric with hand-embroidered letters in
the form of musical instruments, by
Shirley Waxman. Included in the ecu-
menical exhibition "Fabrics of Faith"
held at the National Cathedral in
Washington, D.C., 1992. *Photograph by
Herb Pennock.*

lives have been impacted by the disease. I went to see the quilt last
October with my grandchildren. The perfect fall day was a foil for the
spectacle and emotions of thousands of mourners and sympathizers.
Jessica and Alana were awed to see quilts with baby blankets and
teddy bears sewn on them. Of course there were Jewish quilts included as well. We are represented along with all of the ethnic groups,
races, and religions that make up the American "salad bowl."

Some of the most marvelous Judaica textiles come about because

Figure 3-36
The NAMES Project AIDS Memorial
Quilt, October 1992, on the grounds of
the Washington Memorial. *Photograph
by Pamela Rockland.*

Figure 3-37
Detail of AIDS quilt. *Photograph by
Pamela Rockland.*

Figure 3-38
Detial of AIDS quilt. *Photograph by
Pamela Rockland.*

Figure 3-39
One of six stained-glass-appliqué panels at Young Israel of Brookline Synagogue, depicting an ark containing two identical Torahs. Each has a breast plate with twelve jewel-colored stones based on the garb of the High Priest. *Photograph by Ronald S. Sheinson.*

of the dedication and hard work of synagogue sisterhood groups. A superb example of this is the set of six 45″ × 83″ appliqué panels designed by Diane S. Bloom for the Young Israel of Brookline Synagogue. The project took more than eight years from conception to installation and was worked on by thirty-eight women and supervised and coordinated by Miriam K. Sokoloff. While some congregation members liked the austerity of the plain brick interior of Young Israel's synagogue, others wanted to add beauty to holiness. Now, though, with the six panels installed, the simple *shul* is one of the most spiritual places I know. The panels are based on themes from Israeli stamps. The one shown in Color Plate 17 is Diane Bloom's original design. It is a Torah shaped to resemble a tower-form spice box, which is used at the Havdalah service ending the Sabbath, and includes the multiwick candle flame also used for that ceremony.

When novelist John Updike said, "The past is embedded in the present," he must have been talking about that "noodle pudding," the Jewish People. Whichever diaspora or century we are in, we always remember Jerusalem.

Sheila M. Groman designed and made the quilt "This Year in Jerusalem of Gold" as a gift for her son Kevin, who had his bar mitzvah on top of Masada. The appliquéd, embroidered, and quilted wall hanging is a montage of famous Jerusalem landmarks. Flying over the "City of Peace" is a dove of peace. Sheila writes, "Hopefully, this city of peace will truly be a peaceful city, in a country of peace, a region of peace and a world of peace." See Color Plate 18.

PART FOUR

The Future

Once there was a Momma bird and three baby birds. They
had to cross the sea and a mighty gale came up. The
Momma bird realized that she could only battle the winds if
she carried one bird at a time, so she set out with the first
baby. As she was flying against the wind, holding the baby
bird, she said: "See how I suffer for you, my child, how
hard I work to save your life. When I am old and feeble,
will you take care of me?" "Oh yes, Momma. Surely I will;
just get me to the other side." "You lie," said the Momma,
and dropped the baby bird into the sea.

She went back, picked up the second baby bird and set
out again. Struggling valiantly against the wind she said:
"See how I struggle to save you. When I am old, will you
take care of me?" "Oh yes, Momma," said the baby. "Just
get me to the other side." "You lie," she said, and dropped
the baby bird into turbulent waters.

She went back to the shore and picked up the third baby
and again set out to battle the wind. As before, when she
got to the middle and was most exhausted, she said to the
baby bird: "See how I struggle against the elements for
you. I am so tired, yet I keep going. When I am old and
weak, will you take care of me as I am now taking care of
you?" "Well, Momma," said the third baby bird. "I can't
promise that; times may be different; I don't know. But of
one thing I am sure: whatever you do for me, I will do for
my children." "That was a wise and true answer," said the
Momma bird. "For the sake of my grandchildren I will take
you across the sea."

Adapted from a story told by Gluckel of Hameln in her *Memoirs*

Figure 4-1
"From Generation to Generation," silkscreen print.

From Generation to Generation

In Part Three I quoted John Updike as saying that "the past is embedded in the present." In that same vein, the present is the departure point for the future. What we do now we do for the future. We are the past for future generations. It's easy to be nervous about the future if we listen to the social and political forecasters. My answer to this anxiety, as to most others, is to "sew Jewish." It may not solve *everything,* but it can't hurt!

Yes, sew Jewish: especially for, with, and about children. They are the future.

Figure 4-2
Needlepoint baby picture, 12″ × 16″, designed by Alice Nussbaum, embroidered by Esther Miller. *Photograph by Linhoff Corporate Color.*

Projects: For, With, and About Children

A meaningful folk custom orginated in the Jewish communities of Germany, then spread to parts of France and Italy, and eventually found its way to the descendants of these congregations here in America. The swaddling clothes used at an infant boy's circumcision

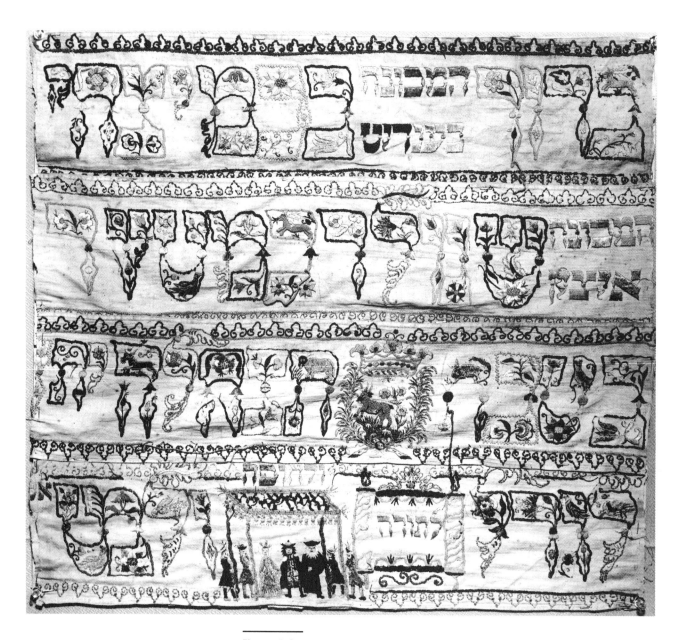

Figure 4-3

Embroidered Torah wrapper (wimple), Germany 1735. From the Danzig Collection at the Jewish Museum, New York City. Picture from the Photographic Archive of the Jewish Theological Seminary of America. *Photograph by Frank J. Darmstaedter.*

ceremony were made into a long wrapper for the Torah scroll, and painted or embroidered with his name, birth date, and wishes for a future of Torah, marriage, and good deeds.

The wrapper, which is wound around the Torah scroll several times and then self-tied, is used to keep the heavy parchment of the scroll from unwinding and breaking. The Torah mantle goes over this. This personalized wrapper, or *wimple* as it was called in German (meaning *banner*,) was used to wrap the Torah on the first day the child was brought to the synagogue, usually at one year of age. It was left on until another was made and then stored until the baby became a bar mitzvah; and it was used again on that occasion. Whether they were stored with the family or the synagogue varied from congregation to congregation.

Figure 4-3 shows an embroidered *wimple* from eighteenth-century Germany; the same wish for a life of Torah, happy marriage, and good deeds, bordered by an alef-bet, was embroidered as a decoration for the baby's room by a loving grandmother in Minnesota (Fig. 4-2).

Fifteen years ago when Wisconsin calligrapher Cindy Pearlman Benjamin was expecting her first child, she made a crib quilt with the same

Figure 4-4
Patch from Ariel Benjamin's crib quilt, by Cindy Benjamin. *Photograph by Kenneth M. Bernstein.*

Figure 4-5
Ariel's crib quilt in progress. *Photograph by Kenneth M. Bernstein.*

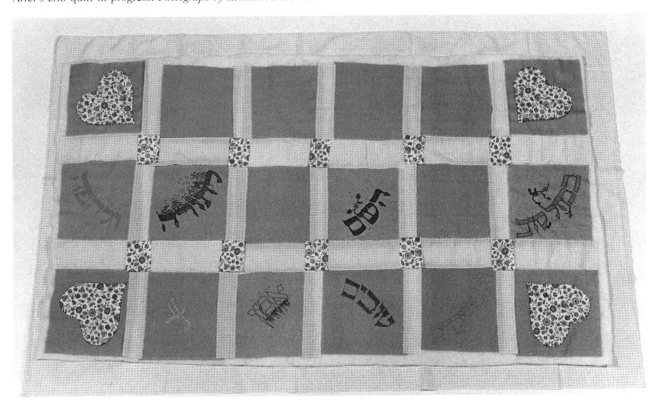

wishes. Cindy designed and drew the words on fourteen 9″ cotton squares. Several friends helped with the embroidery. When the photos in Figs. 4-4 and 4-5 were taken, both quilt and baby were in progress, so the squares with the name and the date could not be filled in. The corner blocks have appliquéd hearts bringing the total number of blocks to eighteen, a lucky number meaning "life." Because the quilt was made with the intention of disassembling it eventually to make

Figure 4-6
Wimple (Torah wrapper) remade from the crib quilt squares in honor of Ariel's bar mitzvah by Cindy Benjamin.

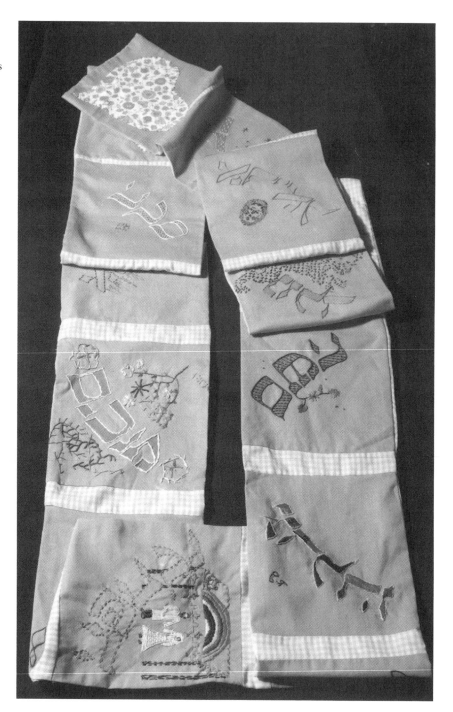

into a *wimple*, it was tied through the small floral sashing squares, rather than quilted.

Eventually, Ariel became a bar mitzvah and his crib quilt was reassembled into a new banner configuration (see Fig. 4-6).

Just as Cindy Benjamin drew on several traditions to make Ariel's *wimple*/quilt, Emma Root did the same in making a sampler to commemorate the birth of her fourth child, Victoria. Unlike Cindy, she is not a calligrapher, but rather a scientist and researcher, and used those considerable skills to design the counted cross-stitch sampler on her computer. The baby girl in the moon is bordered with an alef-bet; the prayer below, in both Hebrew and English, says, "May God inspire you to live in the tradition of Sara, Rebecca, Rachel, and Leah." Emma's computer drawing along with the colors she used is shown in Fig. 4-8. Both she and Victoria have amazing copper-colored hair, so

Figure 4-7
Caroline Victoria's birth sampler by Emma Root.

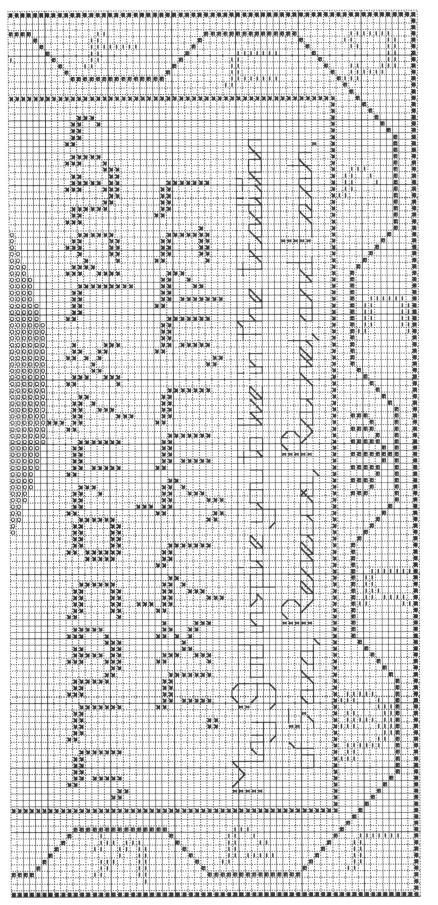

#	Sym	Code	Description
1.	п	334	Baby Blue - med
2.	o	415	Pearl Grey
3.	⊡	437	Tan - lt
4.	■	500	Blue Green - vy dk
5.	✕	501	Blue Green - dk
6.	⋉	760	Salmon
7.	‖	922	Copper - lt

#		Code	Description
8.	·	951	Flesh - lt
9.	⊓	958	Seagreen - dk
10.	◆	3687	Mauve
11.	–	3326	Rose - lt
12.	⊗	3326	Rose - lt
13.	z	3688	Mauve - med
14.	✕	350	Coral - med
15.	⊞	3772	Flesh

Figure 4-8

Computer drawing for the sampler by Emma Root. Reproduced at half size; enlarge 200% to size Emma used.

unless that of your child or grandchild is the same, I'd suggest changing it. Consider changing the other colors to match your baby's room.

Victoria is now at nine the youngest member of our Pomegranate Guild chapter. She has been sewing alongside her mother for years. Using a few simple stitches, she transformed an antique lace doily and napkin into a doll-sized *hallah* cover and tablecloth for "Papa Myron" and "*Tante* Malka." The modified cross-stitch alef-bet shown in Part One, reduced to half-inch size, was used to write the Hebrew phrase "Blessed is the Lord Who Has Sanctified the Sabbath" on the napkin/tablecloth and "*hallah*" on the mini-*hallah* cover. On the small embroidery hoop in the background you can see another tiny *hallah* cover in progress. Figure 4-10 shows the drawing that Victoria followed. She used three stitches: cross-stitch, back stitch, and chain-stitch.

When I began working on this book my granddaughters were eager to help me and it seemed a good time to teach them some new stitches and introduce them to samplers. A number of months earlier Alana had been doodling on my computer and created a drawing that makes up the center of her sampler. We traced it onto the fabric and added her name in both Hebrew and English using the basic cross-stitch alef-bet shown in Part One. I added the Shalom at the top in order to introduce a few more stitches and letters.

Jessica's first sample can be seen in Part One. When she finished, she wanted to do another one, so I drew the design shown in Fig. 4-13

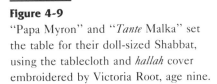

Figure 4-9
"Papa Myron" and "*Tante* Malka" set the table for their doll-sized Shabbat, using the tablecloth and *hallah* cover embroidered by Victoria Root, age nine.

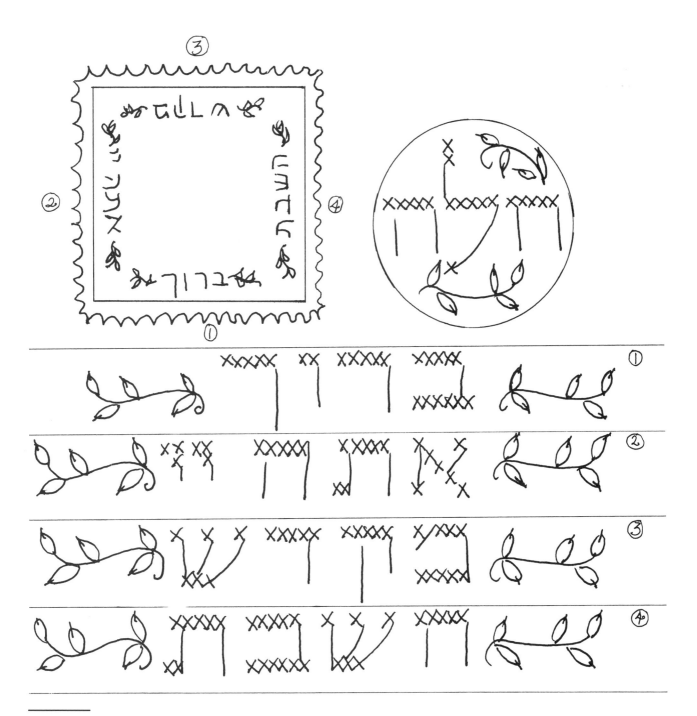

Figure 4-10
Drawing for Victoria Root's tablecloth and *hallah* cover.

for her. She is still working on it and like a true needleworker carries it
with her to work on enroute to ballet lessons.

Almost eight years ago my son David phoned and asked what I'd
like to be called, "Grandma" or "Bubbie." That was how he told us
that we were to be grandparents. Very exciting news! I chose Bubbie,
and the next day I started on a drawing for a quilt for the new baby. By

Figure 4-11
Jessica, five, begins her sampler.
Photograph by the author.

Figure 4-12
Alana's first sampler.

the time I finished, six years later, I had two grandchildren and therefore two quilts. The idea behind my design was that I could carry around with me simple blocks to appliqué and embroider whenever a minute presented itself. The outer border of the quilt represents the created world with fish, flowers, houses, and hearts. The trees at either end of the quilt are shaped like menorahs and have eighteen leaves each, which signify life. The center background is a strip-pieced combination of lilac and light blue to represent the sky and rain. In the center yellow represents the sun. Crowned birds fly around between heaven and earth. Each quilt is made up of sixty-three 8½″ squares (seven squares wide by nine squares long). The surrounding border is 3″ wide. When the two quilt tops were assembled and the blocks sewn together, I lightly drew the quilting plan on them with a pencil and sent them to my Mennonite friend Mary Anne Flaud in Pennsylvania, who arranged to have them quilted with yellow thread to simulate tiny flecks of sunlight (see Color Plate 20).

The two baby quilts for Alana and her sister Jessica grew along

Figure 4-13
Drawing for "*Shalom*" sampler.

Figure 4-14
"In the Beginning," detail of *menorah*-form Tree of Life quilt.

with them into coverings for single beds. After that, I determined that I would not be caught short when my next generation arrived, and with two impending weddings I decided to begin laying in a supply of baby quilts. This gave me the perfect excuse to experiment with a traditional pattern that has long intrigued me called Baby Blocks (or Tumbling Blocks). By playing with different values of colored pencils on a chart of the pattern, I was able to create a design in which seven light stars seem to emerge in a field of floating blocks. The stair-like border was achieved by lining up only light and medium values at the edge and then binding them as the zigzag they created rather than filling in with half blocks to create the more usual straight edge (see Color Plate 19). Although the Star of David, one of the newest Jewish symbols, is so overused that I generally shy away from it in my designs, I reasoned that by manipulating the Baby Blocks pattern to form six-pointed stars I could make a traditional quilt with a Jewish design. Many other quiltmakers have used the pattern to make stars. For instance, the Columbia layout combines a six-pointed star made of two colors with Baby Blocks or cubes set in between the points in such a way that they do not create a three-dimensional effect. The pattern, called Seven Sisters, has equilateral triangles that join large hexagons

Figure 4-15
Layout for the Tree of Life quilt.

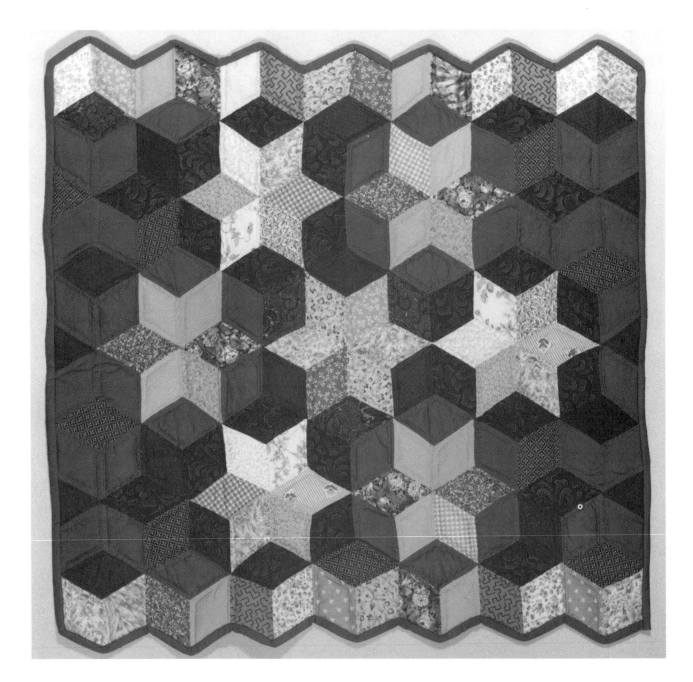

Figure 4-16
"Tumbling Blocks with Emerging Stars," 33″ × 33″, baby carriage quilt.

made of seven stars each. My little quilt is a combination of these two layouts. It's not a new idea, but new for me and fun besides. I plan to continue playing with the Baby Blocks and have some thoughts of embroidering or printing them with the alef-bet or other symbols before joining them. That is for future quilts.

Only one template, that of a 60° diamond, is needed to make most of the quilt. You will also need a 60° equilateral triangle to fill in the top and bottom edges.

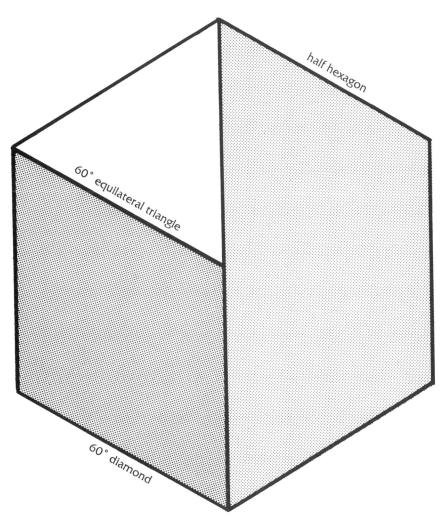

Figure 4-17
All-purpose template for star designs.
Enlarge or reduce as needed.

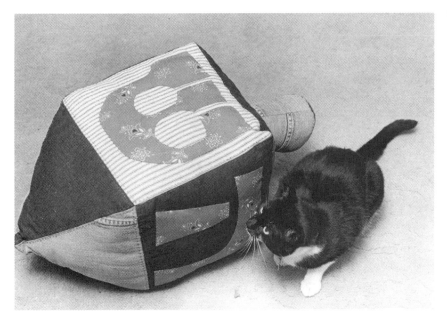

Figure 4-18
Tevya contemplating blue denim
dreidel.

The fact that it took six years to make the two quilts for Alana and Jessica had a wonderful fallout. Whenever I sewed while they were around, invariably they wanted to "help." Even when they were tiny they would hold my hand and help me pull the needle through. In time they graduated to pulling the needle itself and making the odd stitch. My daughter-in-law Pamela found a local shop that sold small remnants of cotton print fabric and she would let the girls pick out whatever they liked. Soon their dolls had quilts and they were teaching their friends to sew. I bought them sewing baskets for their growing collection of tools and trims.

When I sew with Jessica and Alana I feel as though I'm in a time warp. I'm not sure if I am me, or them, or if I am my own grandmother or mother. I never met either of my grandmothers. I knew that my *Bobeh* Raisel died when my father was a child. Listening to the radio news broadcasts during World War II, I would imagine my *Bobeh* Chaya Faigle, having escaped the Nazis, trudging up the hill from the subway so that we could sit and sew, just as I now do with Jessica and Alana.

We had a cat named Tevya for nineteen years. The older he got the more intuitive he became. When he was about fifteen, he developed glaucoma and his eyes swelled horribly. We were told that the only way to save his life would be to remove his eyes. We had the surgery done and brought him home with his familiar face shaved and his eye sockets sewn into Frankenstein scars. He recuperated for a few hours and then was back at his old sports. We found him on the living room rug playing with a mouse he had caught. Ordinarily we would have been properly dismayed and stopped the activity. But eyeless Tevya, faultlessly leaping after the mouse he threw across the room and landing on it by following its invisible trajectory with his "third eye," was positively inspiring. To "see" the future you want and just go for it was the lesson old Tevya taught us.

That is what Tracy Weisman is doing with her young son Adam. Tracy started quilting nearly three years ago, shortly after Adam was born. She had made fifteen quilts so far, and when she saw a news item in the magazine *Quilting Today* announcing that I was looking for Jewish Quilts for this book, she wrote the following description of "Adam's Menorah Quilt":

> Because I converted to Judaism after meeting my husband,
> it took a while for me to feel the Jewish holidays were my
> own. Although I was committed to raising Jewish children
> and having a Jewish home, I quickly discovered that adopt-
> ing an entirely new set of traditions was like looking in a
> mirror and not recognizing myself. It seems so obvious now,
> but it took time for me to realize that observing the Sab-
> bath and Jewish holiday rituals was the best way for my

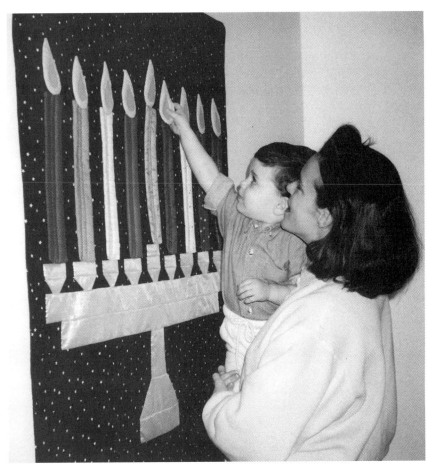

Figure 4-19
Adam Weisman, age three, enjoying
"Adam's Menorah Quilt" with detach-
able Velcro flames. Made by his
mother, Tracy Weisman. *Photograph by
Tony Weisman.*

home—and my heart—to attain a Jewish identity. As someone once said, "In order to *be* Jewish you have to *do*
Jewish." This seems especially true for people who come to
Judaism as adults, whose childhood memories are of another
religion.

I thought of making this quilt in November 1992. I was
trying to think of something I could do that would make
Adam feel he had a special role to play in our family's observance of Hanukkah. Concretely, I was searching for
something to make that I'd bring out once a year at Hanukkah; something that would become a family tradition. . . .

Ironically, my inspiration came as I remembered a wall
hanging my mother made when I was a child that depicted
a partridge in a pear tree. When this familiar item was hung
in our home, Christmas wasn't far behind. Instead of "The
Twelve Days of Christmas," I thought, I'll make "The
Eight Days of Hanukkah."

Once the idea was hatched, I designed the quilt in about
fifteen minutes on graph paper. It was constructed entirely
by machine. The black background fabric with white stars

seemed the perfect choice to represent the darkened night sky of Hanukkah. The *menorah* was constructed of silver lamé, since our family lamp is silver. . . .

The candles and flames are all backed with Velcro. Each night of Hanukkah, Adam chose a candle to affix to the Hanukkah lamp and "lit" it with a fabric flame. Then my husband and I lit the real candles and sang the blessings. Toddlers especially love repetition, and Adam quickly came to look forward to his important part of our holiday celebration. The quilt hung in our kitchen/family room for eight nights; taking it down was an important visual clue to my son that the holiday was over. Eight days is a long time when you are three.

I like to think that the most special part of having made this quilt will come *next* Hanukkah, when I take it out of storage, and a smile of recognition brightens my son's face. . . . We'll tell the story of the brave Maccabees, marvel at the miracle of the lamp that burned for eight days, and hang the menorah quilt together. And, probably, it will smell faintly of oil and fried potato *latkes* from the year before.

At Purim, a delightful end-of-winter holiday, we celebrate the physical deliverance of the Jews of ancient Persia from annihilation at the hands of the wicked Haman. The story of the brave and true heroine, Esther, is told in the Megillah, which is read to the accompaniment of hilarity and noise at the very mention of Haman's name. The Sefardim identified with Esther, and therefore Purim was a very important holiday for them. During the Inquistion, the Marranos, who were afraid to fast at Yom Kippur for fear of being noticed, would fast instead on the Fast of Esther. When my parents were growing up in Eastern Europe, Purim was a much more important event in the Jewish communities than Hanukkah.

It is unlikely that the events in the Purim story occurred as they are related in the Megillah. Historians suggest that the Scheherazade-like Book of Esther was a classical period novel and, like the books of Judith and Daniel, written as underground literature to keep up the people's spirit during the turbulent Second Temple period.

Many things that never happened however, are true. We may see the Book of Esther as an allegory that explains and transforms universal end-of-winter customs much older than itself into a celebration of deliverance from physical destruction. (Carnival and St. Patrick's Day share many of Purim's characteristics.) That doesn't make it less meaningful. Throughout our long history there have been more than enough Hamans to justify a holiday when one is encouraged to become so drunk that one can no longer differentiate between the evil

Haman and the good Mordecai. If you survive, that's reason enough for a party!

Masks and costumes for children and adults are as much a part of the Purim holiday as buffoonery, wine, and *hamentaschen* (triangular, filled cookies or pastries resembling Haman's hat). Artist Deborah Kelman made a series of Purim masks that are as compelling as any of her other textile pieces. When I called to ask her permission to try my hand at a fast and easy version of the masks, she was delighted and told me about her carved foam rubber *hamentasch* bodysuit. Although not strictly a fabric piece (only the "filling" is a red calico fabric), we decided to include it here. Foam rubber pads were carved with an electric knife to the appropriate shape and a stuffed filling was made with the printed red fabric. The front and back are joined at the shoulders, armpits, and crotch with Velcro tabs.

To make the mask shown in Fig. 4-21 start with a 9″ × 12″

Figure 4-20
"Queen Esther," handmade felt mask, 15″ × 16″, by Deborah Kelman. *Photograph courtesy of the artist.*

Figure 4-21
Wearable qwik-felt "Haman" mask. Inspired by an 18″ × 28″ sculpted felt mask by Deborah Kelman.

Figure 4-22
Drawing for Haman mask to enlarge and embellish as desired.

Figure 4-23
"Haman" (alias Larry Kaplan) coaxing his son David into foam and fabric *hamentasch* costume by Deborah Kelman.

rectangle of fabric (I used charcoal gray felt). With chalk draw the triangular shape of the mask and position the eyes according to the size of the eventual wearer. Cut the edges of the fabric into narrow strips up to the chalk triangle to create the beard. Knotting some of the strips adds character. A piece of red fabric was sewn into the mouth opening to form a pocket where buttons were glued for the teeth. The nostrils are cut open and the long nose folded and sewn on the fold line to shape the mask. Wide machine satin stitches were used to outline the eyes in red and the nose in black. A black ribbon was twisted and sewn in place for the single sinister eyebrow. The project took about an hour to complete and was a lot of fun. When choosing a color for the mask, consider using fabric close to the wearer's hair color as this adds a certain realism.

When Miriam Sokoloff and her family received the invitation to Baruch Sheinson's Purim bar mitzvah, it provided another avenue for Miriam's creativity. She decided that an autographed quilt would be a unique bar mitzvah gift, and set about planning one with a Purim theme. Triangles, in *hamentasch* colors, lent themselves perfectly to this plan, and before going to the bar mitzvah, she cut out 3″ triangles of brown, gold, and rust calicoes as well as triangles of a light-colored print fabric to be autographed. She also added a number of Pilot brand ultra-fine-point permanent SC-UF markers in brown to her quilt-on-the-road-bundle.

At the *seudah* (festive meal) following the Megillah reading, the five Sokoloffs visited all the tables and asked the guests to each sign a triangular patch of the light-colored print fabric. Later in the day everyone helped arrange the calico triangles in an alternating pattern with the signed ones. Miriam then enlarged the invitation design, copied it onto rust-colored fabric, and then embroidered it with off-

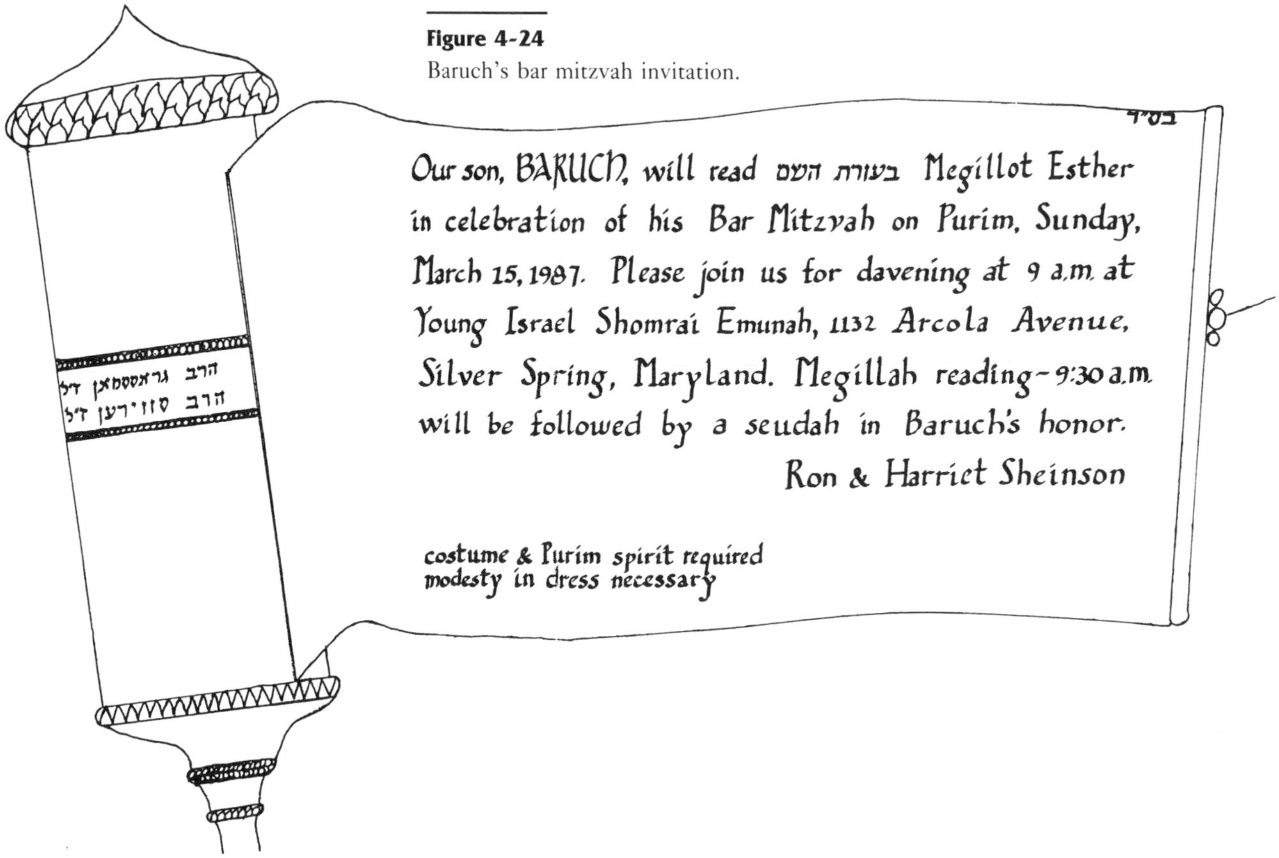

Figure 4-24
Baruch's bar mitzvah invitation.

Our son, BARUCH, will read בעזרת השם Megillot Esther in celebration of his Bar Mitzvah on Purim, Sunday, March 15, 1987. Please join us for davening at 9 a.m. at Young Israel Shomrai Emunah, 1132 Arcola Avenue, Silver Spring, Maryland. Megillah reading—9:30 a.m. will be followed by a seudah in Baruch's honor.

Ron & Harriet Sheinson

costume & Purim spirit required
modesty in dress necessary

Figure 4-25
Baruch's *hamentasch* quilt, 54 × 46″.

white embroidery floss. Using waste canvas and large cross-stitch block letters she embroidered the following within the open Megillah:

Bar Mitzvah
Baruch
Purim
5747

The triangles were machine pieced, along with the embroidered center, to form the quilt top. It was then layered with batting and backing and tied with the "tails" on the back of the quilt.

We wish a new baby a life of Torah, *huppah*, and good deeds. Babies quickly grow to become bat and bar mitzvah and before you know it, you're planning weddings. One proverb says that at five your child is your master; at ten your slave; at fifteen your double; and after that he or she is your friend or foe—depending on how you raised him or her. Another proverb tells us that "your child may be a robber, yet you dance at his wedding" (Leo Rosten's *Treasury of Jewish Quotations*). The weddings we participate in now will create the families of the future, which will, in turn, carry the past forward even as they create new traditions.

Jewish wedding customs vary throughout the world. In ancient Greece, a Jewish bride and groom wore wreaths of foliage as crowns; in Roman times, lighted torches were used in procession. In Spain, Jews once married only under a new moon; in Germany only under a full moon. The folk custom of the groom breaking a glass after the benedictions have been said has been popular for centuries and has many interpretations. Some say it commemorates the destruction of the Temple in 70 C.E.; others say that it is a reminder that all happiness is transient. For others breaking a glass is thought to bring good luck to the marriage and to help keep it intact.

The *huppah* (wedding canopy) also has many traditions and interpretations. The idea of being married under a wedding canopy probably goes back to the tent or chamber of the bridegroom in which the marriage was consummated (Joel 2:16; Psalms 19:5–6). The groom and bride are each brought to the *huppah* by both of their parents. Today it symbolizes the new home the couple is about to establish. It is a piece of fabric fastened at the corners to four poles and is often held by friends or family members, although sometimes stationary canopies are used. The *huppah* is often decorated with stars and moons, signifying that the marriage takes place with heavenly sanction, with psalms and with quotations from the seven wedding benedictions. A handmade *tallit* is a simple and dramatic choice for a wedding canopy.

In ancient Judea it was customary to plant a pine tree when a girl was born and a cedar tree when a boy was born. When they were married, the wedding canopy was made of the interwoven branches from both trees (Talmud, *Gittin*, 57a). In today's Israel the custom has grown of using a *tallit* supported by rifles rather than poles.

I am asked for *huppah* designs more than for any other Judaica object, both for synagogues and for individuals. I don't know if this is universally true for my fellow textile artists, but judging from the photographs and slides that were sent to me for this book, I imagine that it may be the same for them. See Color Plates 21 and 22 for two particularly noteworthy contemporary *huppot*.

Figure 4-26
Tallit/huppah, wool, cotton, silk, metallic fibers; bamboo poles with ribbon and abalone shells, by Temma Gentles. *Photograph by Gilbert.*

Oregon textile artist Phyllis Kantor is primarily known as a weaver. To make the *huppah* entitled "*Ani L'Dodi*," she collaborated with calligrapher Reeva Kimble, who designed the lettering and then wove the fabric, quilted the flowers, and embellished it with embroidery detailing and beads.

Paula Nadelstern is well known in quilting circles. She was the New York State winner of the first and second Great American Quilt contests, a biennial event of the Museum of American Folk Art in

Figure 4-27
Huppah for Congregation Beth El, Birmingham, Michigan, by Temma Gentles. The Huppah is designed to extend the view through the perimeter windows in this sanctuary by architect Minoru Yamasaki. The tree motif reminds us of the custom of planting a tree when a child is born and using the boughs at his/her marriage. A pomegranate and fig tree spread their branches over the couple. *Photograph by the artist.*

Figure 4-28
Wedding scene at Holy Blossom Temple, Toronto, Ontario. Temma Gentles' *Huppah* features rainbow streamers lettered with part of the seventh wedding benediction.

New York City. She writes, "I make quilts on the block in the Bronx where I grew up. Being a New Yorker wrapped up in the fabric of city life creates an inherent paradox that contrasts the traditional image of quiltmaking as part of a simple, make-do, rural way of life with my own complex urban-shaped space. Because I connect to its methods and material with passion, I choose quiltmaking to translate my skills and personality into visual expression. I am personally delighted by quilts which lead the audience toward a multi-layered point of view. . . . I am intrigued by the structure of fabricated kaleidoscopes. . . ." "Kaleidoscope IV: The Crystal Canopy" is part of series of kaleidoscope quilts. In it Paula not only develops her mysterious fractured and mirrored imagery, but makes exquisite use of the challenging *magen David* symbol. When used as a *huppah*, the quilt was attached to supporting poles with Velcro loops.

The *huppah* shown in Fig. 4-29 uses a phrase from the seven benedictions—"Let the Heaven's Rejoice and the Earth Be Glad"— as well as flowers, birds, and stars to signify heaven and earth. It was made to be displayed as a decorative banner at the Elmont Jewish

Figure 4-29
"Let the Heavens Rejoice and the Earth Be Glad," wool and cotton appliquéd *huppah* for Elmont Jewish Center, New York.

Center in New York in-between weddings. The banner can be hung by threading a short drapery rod through its loops at the top. When in use as a *huppah* the loops serve as a decorative fringe. Four grommet-reinforced holes at the corners allow decorative wooden finials to screw into the supporting poles. This is the second version of this *huppah* made for the Elmont Jewish Center. It was created to take the place of the first one, which was "lost" or stolen.

An increasingly widespread custom is to make your own *huppah*. The *huppah* becomes an instant heirloom whether it is stored afterward to be reused at other family weddings or used as a wall hanging or

Figure 4-30
Paper-cut *ketuba* (wedding contract), by Naomi Hordes with calligraphy by Linda
Katzper. *Photograph by Joel Breger Assoc.*

bed quilt in the new couple's home. The paper-cut borders of the *ketuba* (wedding contract) shown in Fig. 4-30 were designed and made by Maryland artist Naomi Hordes for her daughter's wedding in June 1992. The text is the traditional Aramaic document lettered by calligrapher Linda Katzper. Naomi comes from an intensely observant and Zionist background and has had a lifelong interest and training in art. Thus it was only natural for her to make not only the *ketuba* for her daughter's wedding but a hand appliquéd *huppah* as well.

The canopy, which is supported by a fabric-covered PVC frame, consists of four panels and a top section. The panels contain the quotation from Psalms 137:6: "We will elevate Jerusalem above our chief joys." The front panel shows scenes of Jerusalem in addition to symbols of fecundity such as pomegranates, fish, and grapes. The top of the *huppah* has traditional wedding blessings and good luck omens as well as the couple's logo, designed by the bride, on it. The Hordes

Figure 4-31

Huppah and wedding tablecloth, hand appliquéd by Naomi Hordes.
Photograph by Joel Breger Assoc.

family hopes that over the generations their descendants will add to the *huppah*. The design is executed in richly colored felt on upholstery fabric. A matching tablecloth to hold wine goblets and a zippered pocket, with the quotation "In remembrance of the destruction of the Temple," to hold the glass to be broken at the end of the ceremony complete the *huppah*.

As mentioned previously, my two youngest children were married this past year. Keren and Matt's *huppah* was an elegant but simple to make confection of three banquet-size commercially available hand crocheted lace tablecloths, held to a wooden frame with wire and flowers. Jeffrey and Liana indulged my desire to assemble a family album quilt for their wedding. (Years earlier my oldest son David had used his *tallit* as the *huppah* at his wedding to Pam.)

With thoughts of continuity and heirlooms in mind, I undertook Jeffrey and Liana's *huppah* quilt in fall 1991 in preparation for their wedding the following July.

After talking with Jeff and Liana and finding out what size they would like the quilt to be (queen-size) and what their preferred colors were, I made a layout plan for the blocks, having decided beforehand that I did not want to do the quilt in traditional squares. The blocks were cut into 10¼" hexagons from blue fabric (measuring from flat side to flat side; point to point the hexagons were 12"). This included the ¼" seam allowance. (Enlarge the all-purpose template for star designs in Fig. 4-17 to the size you want.) Jeffrey and Liana had sent me a list

Figure 4-32
"Mazel Tov" huppah quilt, detail.

Figure 4-33
"Mazel Tov" huppah quilt, layout.

of people who they hoped would want to participate in their *huppah* quilt and I sent each of them a kit containing the following letter, which gave directions on how to proceed, the block fabric, and assorted pieces of coordinating fabrics for those who wanted to appliqué. I hope the letter will help you plan your own group quilt (see Color Plate 23 for the completed quilt).

October 20, 1991

Liana and Jeff's *"Mazel Tov" Huppah* Quilt

Dear Folks:

In July of 1992 we will celebrate the marriage of Jeffrey and Liana. Following Jewish tradition the ceremony will take place under a *huppah* (wedding canopy), which represents the couple's new home. Jeff and Liana's huppah has been designed to be used after the ceremony as a queen-size bed quilt. We hope that it will give them many years of warmth, comfort, and love from all of us who participate in making it. Twenty special patches plus borders make up the design. Each of the patches will be embellished by family and friends of Jeff and Liana.

According to Jewish Folk Tradition, a marriage takes place under the "eyes of Heaven," which are the stars. Therefore, a star theme was chosen for the quilt and a star-patterned fabric selected for its lining. The overall configuration of the blocks forms a pattern of interlocking stars. Since each of the star's center hexagon-shaped blocks will be worked by a different family member, the design, as well as the work on the quilt, also represents the joining together of our families. The Hebrew word for constellation is *Mazel*. We wish Liana and Jeffrey "*Mazel Tov*," "Congratulations!" A Good Constellation on their marriage and throughout their life together. (Among Spanish Jews, the expression "*Mazzal Alto*," a "high constellation," is also used with the same congratulatory meaning.)

How To Proceed

Embroider or appliqué your block with a design, symbol, motif, picture, poem, or idea that reflects your wishes for, or relationship with, Jeff or Liana or both of them. Some suggestions to trigger your imagination might be favorite or shared foods, music, events, humor, or seasons.

- Draw the design on paper first and then transfer it to the block using the enclosed dressmaker's tracing paper, or draw lightly with chalk. (Do not use ordinary carbon paper as it will permanently soil the fabric.)
- *Please* sign your patch. Embroider your signature or initials as part of the design or in a corner. The date isn't necessary since one of the blocks will be a date block.
- Keep your design ½"–¾" from the edges to allow for seams.
- Use embroidery thread in the following colors only: [colors chosen to match the selected fabrics]
- Use the enclosed scrap of floral fabric as your color guide. If you wish, *use* the fabric to appliqué part of your patch. Also enclosed are pieces of other corresponding fabrics for you to use in your design if you desire. Use one or more or none.

Please Return the Finished Patch by December 20th, 1991

- If you cannot participate, please return the patch to me immediately so that I can have someone else work on it.
- When all of the patches have been returned, I will arrange and assemble them and then have the completed top hand quilted in Pennsylvania. So you see, we need *time*!!

I am looking forward so much to seeing Jeff and Liana under this *huppah* and to sharing this joyous event with all of you.

Best regards,
Mae

Only two people were not able to participate and their patches were quickly reassigned. The patches from relatives on my side of the family trickled in one at a time. It's always exciting to see what Grandma Bess or Aunt Linda had come up with. Most of Liana's family, on the other hand, live close to one another in Winnipeg, Canada, so my *machetenesteh* (a Yiddish word that defines the relationship between the two mothers-in-law, *consuegra* in Spanish) Ruth Condello, who is a multitalented craftsperson, arranged a family sewing bee, which resulted in a delightful pile of ten appliquéd, trapuntoed, and embroidered patches that arrived all at once.

A queen-size quilt is rather enormous to hold on four poles as a *huppah*. Ruth came up with the idea of rolling the borders, holding them in place, and festooning them with ribbons.

Figure 4-34
Pattern for "Hand and Heart Will Never Part." This message from a Victorian valentine was mine to Jeffrey and Liana.

At the wedding we finally got to meet the folks we had been
sewing with long distance and somehow we already felt like family.
After the ceremony, the *huppah* was disassembled and spread out on a
large table at the reception party that followed the ceremony. Jeffrey
and Liana had prepared a booklet describing the different patches and
listing who their makers were. As we circled around the *huppah*
identifying patches with people, it was a satisfying and warm way to
get to know our new relatives.

As I said at the beginning of this book, "God Made Man because He
Loves Stories." And the story keeps circling around and repeating
itself, with endless variations created by the human mind and spirit.
What message should we send into the future? I can think of none
better than the dictum of Reb Nachman of Bratslov, which Leila
Abelow embroidered as a gift for her daughter and son-in-law: "It Is a
Great *mitzvah* [commandment/good deed/blessing] to Always Be
Happy." Loosely translated it means "It is a blessing to be happy
forever." It is not easy to always be happy, but it certainly is worth the
effort and is far better than the alternative.

Leila's grandparents were totally observant in the Orthodox man-
ner. Her mother rebelled, so Leila was raised in a Jewish but subur-
ban-secular environment. In turn, Leila wanted more substance in her
family life and so created what she calls an "anthropological-tradi-
tional" environment for her children. Now we come full circle. Leila's
daughter, son-in-law, and grandchildren are once again totally Orthodox. Leila wanted to make something special for them to hang over
the sofa, something that would express her joy in life and love for her
family. She brought me Reb Nachman's quotation and described her
children's very devout life-style. Not wanting to depict the clichéd

Figure 4-35
"It is a Great *Mitzvah* to Always Be Happy," (Reb Nachman of Bratslov).

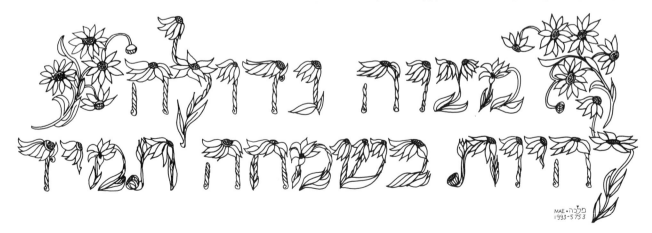

version of happiness, the dancing Hasid, we played with the notion of dancing letters. It was at this time that I was working on transforming the flea-market daisy doily into a *hallah* cover, and the notion of a flower alef-bet fell into place as the perfect way to interpret Reb Nachman's proverb. Leila's exuberance for the project is expressed in her delicious use of color.

Go, children, and be happy.

DIRECTORY OF JUDAICA TEXTILE ARTISTS

The artists listed below can be commissioned to design and make a variety of Jewish ceremonial and decorative textiles. Many of them will just create the design, allowing you to do the needlework. Some are also available for lectures and workshops.

Leah Allman
    75 Harrison Avenue
    Peabody, MA 01960

Abby Block
    1550 Ryders Lane
    Highland Park, IL 60035

Lonnie Stern Boninger
    707 N. McKean Street
    Butler, PA 16001

Lydie Egosi Studio
    100 West 57th Street
    New York, NY 10019

Temma Gentles
    22 Inglewood Drive
    Toronto, Ontario M4T IG8

Ina Golub
    366 Rolling Rock Road
    Mountainside, NJ 07092

Sheila Minkin Groman
    14417 Futura Drive
    Sun City West, AZ 85375

Rita Lenkin Hawkins
    11603 Terrytown Drive
    Reisterstown, MD 21136

Naomi Hordes
    9507 Midwood Road
    Silver Spring, MD 20910

Phyllis Kantor
    1948 Kimberly Drive
    Eugene, OR 97405

Deborah Kelman
    901 Schooner Street
    Foster City, CA 94404

Margery and Eli Langner
    25 St. Nicholas Street
    Lynbrook, NY 11563

Larosh
    18744 Parthenia #1
    Northridge, CA 91324

Lynne Lederman
    P.O. Box 651
    Shrewsbury, MA 01545

Peachy Levy
    500 East Channel Road
    Santa Monica, CA 90402

Paula Nadelstern
    98 Van Cortland Park South
    Bronx, NY 10463

Alice Nussbaum
    25 Crandon Way
    Rochester, NY 14618

Jeanette Kuvin Oren
    6104 Crossover Lane
    Rockville, MD 20852

Pamela Rishfeld
    4467 Terracemeadow Court
    Moorpark, CA 93021

Emma Root
201 West Main Street
Westborough, MA 01581

Dona Rosenblatt
2428 Valley Forge
Richardson, TX 75080

Ruth Rubin
4949 Genesta, Apt. 414
Encino, CA 91316

Florette S. Semigran
20379 W. Country Club
Drive, #2640
Aventura, FL 33180

Miriam K. Sokoloff
21 Hancock Road
Brookline, MA 02146

Corine Soikin Strauss
237 W. Mount Airy Road
Croton-on-Hudson, NY
10520

Mae Rockland Tupa
Myron Tupa
Metatron Designs
106 Francis Street
Brookline, MA 02146

Shirley Waxman
7531 Coddle Harbor Lane
Potomac, MD 20854

Bonnie Yales
248 Bishops Forest
Waltham, MA 02154

The following organizations support the growth of Judaic textile arts and can help you make connections for classes, teachers, or commissionable artists in your area.

The American Guild of Judaic Art
P.O. Box 1794
Murray Hill Station
New York, NY 10156-0609

ArtSites, The Jewish Artists' Cooperative
Roz Houseknecht,
Executive Director
12116 Hunters Lane
Rockville, MD 20852

J.A.C.O.B. (Jewish Artists & Craftspeople of the Bay)
1414 Walnut Street
Berkeley, CA 94789

The Jewish Folk Arts Society
11710 Hunters Lane
Rockville, MD 20852

The Pomegranate Guild of Judaic Needlework
3316 Longridge Terrace
Sherman Oaks, CA 91423

BIBLIOGRAPHY

Adi-Rubin. *Israeli Yemenite Embroidery*. Seattle: Cone-Heiden, 1983.

Davis, Eli and Elise. *Jewish Folk Art Over the Ages*. Jerusalem: Rubin Mass, 1977.

Encyclopedia Judaica. Jerusalem: Keter, 1972.

Frankel, Ellen, and Betsy Platkin Teutsch. *The Encyclopedia of Jewish Symbols*. Northvale, N.J.: Jason Aronson, 1992.

Fredman, Ruth Gruber. *The Passover Seder*, Afikomen *in Exile*. Philadelphia: University of Pennsylvania Press, 1981.

Freehof, Lillian S., and Bucky King. *Embroideries and Fabrics for Synagogue and Home*. New York: Hearthside Press, 1966.

Gluckel. *The Memoirs of Gluckel of Hameln*. Translated by Marvin Lowenthal. New York: Schocken Books, 1977.

Marks, Cara Goldberg. *The Handbook of Hebrew Calligraphy*. Northvale, N.J.: Jason Aronson, 1990.

Mann, Dodds, and Glick, eds. *Convivencia: Jews, Muslims, and Christians in Medieval Spain*. New York: George Braziller & The Jewish Museum, 1992.

Polacco, Patricia. *The Keeping Quilt*. New York: Simon & Schuster, 1988.

Rockland, Mae Shafter. *The Work of Our Hands: Jewish Needlecraft for Today*. New York: Schocken Books, 1973.

Salomon, Kathryn. *Jewish Ceremonial Embroidery*. London: B T. Batsford, 1988.

Springer, Selma, and Friends. *Designs of Judaica*. Santa Monica, Calif.: Simcha, 1986.

INDEX